ICE TIME

Young women play on an outdoor
rink in the 1930s. Women have played
hockey for as long as men have.

Left: Tim Horton has been called the strongest man to ever play in the NHL. He was a tough, reliable defenseman who helped the Toronto Maple Leafs to win four Stanley Cups in the 1960s. Horton was traded to the New York Rangers in 1970 and then drafted by the Buffalo Sabres in 1972. While he was driving back home to Buffalo after a game against the Leafs in 1974, Horton crashed his car and was killed. The chain of donut shops that he began when he was with the Leafs still bears his name.

Opposite page: Wayne Gretzky was on skates almost as soon as he could walk. Even as a preschooler, the pride of Brantford had his stick on the ice, ready to make a play.

MICHAEL McKINLEY

THE STORY OF HOCKEY

ICE TIME

TUNDRA BOOKS

For my daughter, Rose, the first star
in a league of her own. – MM

Copyright © 2006 by Canadian Broadcasting Corporation

Published in Canada by Tundra Books
75 Sherbourne Street, Toronto, Ontario M5A 2P9

Published in the United States by Tundra Books of Northern New York
P.O. Box 1030, Plattsburgh, New York 12901

Library of Congress Control Number: 2005911187

Library and Archives Canada Cataloguing in Publication

McKinley, Michael.
    Ice time : the story of hockey / Michael McKinley.

Includes index.
Based on the CBC television series: Hockey: a people's history.
ISBN-13: 978-0-88776-762-3
ISBN-10: 0-88776-762-1

    1. Hockey–History. I. Title.

GV846.5.M2515 2006   796.962'09   20059077654

We acknowledge the financial support of the Government of Canada through the Book Publishing
Industry Development Program (BPIDP) and that of the Government of Ontario through the Ontario
Media Development Corporation's Ontario Book Initiative. We further acknowledge the support of the
Canada Council for the Arts and the Ontario Arts Council for our publishing program.

ONTARIO ARTS COUNCIL
CONSEIL DES ARTS DE L'ONTARIO

Design: Kong Njo

Printed and bound in China

1 2 3 4 5 6   11 10 09 08 07 06

During the 1920s and early 1930s,
Canadian students at England's famous
Oxford University made up the Oxford
ice hockey team. It became one of the
most successful hockey dynasties ever.
Each Christmas, the Oxford team toured
Europe, regularly defeating opponents
by lopsided scores. Some of Canada's
most honored citizens played for Oxford.
Lester B. Pearson went on to become
Canada's fourteenth prime minister.
He is pictured here (in white, right
foreground) in 1922-23 playing
with Oxford against a Swiss team
in Switzerland.

Contents

CHAPTER ONE   7
Game On!

CHAPTER TWO   13
Hockey's First Superstar

CHAPTER THREE   21
Blood and Ice

CHAPTER FOUR   27
Canada's Team

CHAPTER FIVE   35
The Rocket's Red Glare

CHAPTER SIX   41
The National Birthday Party

CHAPTER SEVEN   49
Us & Them

CHAPTER EIGHT   57
The Great One

CHAPTER NINE   65
Mario and Manon

CHAPTER TEN   73
Gold in the Ice

Acknowledgments   79
Index   79
Photo Credits   80

This picture of McGill University's first hockey team is the earliest known photograph of a hockey team. It was taken at Montreal's Crystal Palace Skating Rink on February 28, 1881, just six years after the world's first indoor hockey game was played in Montreal's Victoria Rink.

CHAPTER ONE

Game On!

"A" game of hockey will be played at the Victoria Skating Rink this evening between two nines chosen from among the members. Good fun may be expected as some of the players are reported to be exceedingly excellent at the game."

Anyone who read this announcement in the *Montreal Gazette* on March 3, 1875, had no way of knowing that this game would change history. But taking the game indoors was a bold new move.

The game was organized by James Creighton, a sportsman and engineer who had come to Montreal from Halifax, Nova Scotia. Creighton and his friends played a game in which each team had nine players. All nine played the entire sixty-minute game with just a short break in the middle. There would be no substitutions and no spare players. They wore skates they attached to their boots. Their sticks were made in Nova Scotia by Miq'Mak woodworkers. Their uniforms were rugby jerseys, shorts, and long woolen stockings. They wore no protective padding at all.

Right: James Creighton (second from right, wearing a cap) poses with the Rideau Rebels, an Ottawa hockey club, in 1889. Creighton was one of hockey's founding fathers. After he staged the world's first indoor hockey game in Montreal, he moved to Ottawa, and played on this team with two of the sons of Lord Stanley.

Opposite: The Starr Manufacturing Company of Dartmouth, Nova Scotia, sold millions of skates around the world from 1863 to 1939. In this advertisement from the early twentieth century, the player wears new Starr skates that featured lighter weight and better support for the foot – crucial for the quick twists and turns of hockey.

"YE GOOD OLD DAYS"

Not even goalies wore padding. They had to stand to stop the puck – they were not allowed to drop to their knees. Unlike the modern rubber puck, their "puck" was a wooden disk. Their goal was different, too. It was just a pair of metal posts set into the ice eight feet apart. Creighton's rules were based on the rules for rugby, so players were not allowed to advance down the ice ahead of the puck carrier, or they would be ruled offside.

James Creighton, cheered on by some forty friends and onlookers, captained his team to a 2-1 victory. It was a significant moment in the history of hockey. Before this night, hockey had been a casual, winter game, played on frozen ponds and fields. When James Creighton brought it inside under lights, he opened up the possibility that hockey could be an organized indoor sport watched by spectators in relative comfort. The game would never be the same.

Hockey comes from the ball and stick games that people have been playing for thousands of years. Our modern game took shape because of the cold, northern winters, the invention of the ice skate, and the influence of immigrants from Europe who may have brought their ball-and-stick games to Canada with them.

And then, along came the Queen's man in Canada to give hockey a prize. Governor-General Lord Stanley became a hockey fan as soon as he arrived in Canada in 1888. Two of his sons played on the Rideau Rebels hockey team. (James Creighton played for the Rebels, too.) Even Isobel, Lord Stanley's teenage daughter, played hockey. She was one of the first young women in Ottawa to play in a league.

Above: The Winged Wheelmen of Montreal's Amateur Athletic Association play a match in Montreal's Victoria Rink in 1893. The spectators stand right at the edge of the ice, with no protection from flying pucks. The Wheelmen won the first Stanley Cup.

The First Pro Hockey League: Doc Gibson was a talented athlete who starred at football, soccer, and hockey in his hometown of Berlin (now Kitchener), Ontario. After graduating from dental school in Detroit, Michigan, he began his dental practice in northern Michigan. In 1904, Gibson and local businessmen formed the International Hockey League – the world's first professional hockey league.

In March 1892, Lord Stanley offered to donate a trophy to the great game of hockey. It was to be called the Dominion Challenge Trophy, but soon both fans and players came to know and covet it as the Stanley Cup. Lord Stanley hoped that his "challenge" trophy would help to unite a huge country by bringing teams together from far-flung places. It's probably safe to say that he never imagined what Joe Boyle had in mind.

After graduating from high school in Ontario, Joe Boyle went to New York to join his father and brothers in the horse-racing business. But this wasn't exciting enough for him so, at age seventeen, he quit to go to sea. He sailed around the world, surviving tropical storms and near-shipwrecks. He once fought off a shark with a knife to save the life of a fellow sailor.

But Joe Boyle wanted to be rich, and, like thousands of others, he traveled to the Yukon when gold was found there in the 1890s. By the time he was thirty years old he had made his first million dollars. He used some of the money to build an arena in Dawson City, where teams made up of civil servants and adventurers could play hockey. Joe didn't play himself: he was a promoter. While he was on a business trip to Ottawa he came up with a brilliant idea: he would transport an all-star team – the Dawson City Nuggets – from the Yukon to play the mighty Ottawa Senators for the Stanley Cup.

Above: Lord Stanley became Canada's sixth governor-general in 1888. He soon fell in love with hockey and, in 1892, gave the game the trophy that would come to define hockey excellence: the Dominion Challenge Trophy, better known as the Stanley Cup.

Not Wanted: In the fall of 1893, the Montreal Hockey Club won hockey's newest trophy: Lord Stanley's "Dominion Challenge Trophy." But there was a problem. The Montreal Hockey Club had always practiced at the city's Crystal or Victoria rinks. When they became the first team to win Lord Stanley's trophy, they were representing the Montreal Amateur Athletic Association (MAAA). But they had no voice in the official affairs of the MAAA, and now they resented the MAAA trying to piggyback on their glory. The Stanley Cup's trustees, or caretakers, tried to patch things up by going to Montreal to present the trophy to the Montreal Hockey Club, but no one from that organization showed up to accept. So the MAAA happily accepted it for them. The notes taken by the club secretary record that "The public was never informed of the dispute." So the first Stanley Cup was won by a committee, in secret.

A group of men, called trustees, had been appointed to decide who played for the trophy. Surprisingly, in answer to Boyle's suggestion, they said yes. This was a bit like a team of part-time players from a small town taking on the best NHL team today. The Nuggets were not even regional champions.

So why did the trustees agree to the game? Hockey had lost a number of its best players to a new professional league in the United States; it needed something to catch the attention of the country. And there was money to be made, both by Joe Boyle and other team owners, when the Nuggets toured other towns after the game in Ottawa.

Before they could play, the Dawson City team first had to get to Ottawa – a 4,000-mile trek in the dead of winter. But there had been an unusual warm spell so, first, the team tried to bicycle to Skagway to catch their ferry to Vancouver. When the weather got even warmer, the roads became mush, so they walked. Then winter came back, and the Nuggets were trapped by blizzards. They spent Christmas Eve, 1904, in a shed fifty miles outside of Whitehorse. Their ferry was delayed by fog, and the seasick Nuggets were exhausted when they finally arrived on land. And then they had to travel across the country by train.

The Nuggets made it into Ottawa just two days before the match – on Friday the thirteenth. Newspapers had cheered

With His Eye on the Puck:
He became known as "One-Eyed" Frank McGee after he lost his left eye in a game in 1900, but he went on to become one of early hockey's scoring stars. He led the Ottawa Hockey Club to four Stanley Cup titles. McGee scored fourteen goals in the 23-2 pasting of the Dawson City Nuggets – a record that still stands. Despite having just one good eye, McGee was allowed to join the Canadian army in the First World War, and was killed in combat in September 1916.

Left: The Dawson City Nuggets pose with their manager, Joseph Boyle (center), in Ottawa in 1905. The Nuggets traveled thousands of miles from the gold fields of the Yukon in search of Stanley Cup silver in the nation's capital. Although they were defeated by the mighty Ottawa Silver Seven, the Nuggets' quest captured the imagination of the country. Goalie Albert Forrest (front left), just seventeen years old, was singled out for his fine play in net.

All-Sport All-Star: Dan Bain was one of early hockey's first stars, but like so many other players at the time, was excellent at other sports, too. When he was thirteen, he won a three-mile race to become the roller-skating champion of Manitoba. At seventeen, he took first prize in the city's gymnastics competition. And at twenty, he won the first of three consecutive cycling championships. Bain would add a pairs figure-skating crown, medals in lacrosse and snowshoeing, and the Dominion trapshooting championship. He joined the Winnipeg Victorias hockey team in 1895 by answering an ad in a local newspaper. He made the team in the first five minutes of the tryout. The only thing wrong was his stick, which was held together by wire: the Victorias took it away from him. In February 1896, the team – led by Bain – won the Stanley Cup.

them on their way, and the nation's capital was buzzing with anticipation. These amateurs from the frozen north stood no chance against the Stanley Cup champions and their star player, Frank McGee.

McGee had led the Ottawa Senators to their first Stanley Cup in 1903, and he and the team went on to defend the Cup a remarkable eight times before he retired after the 1905-06 season. They became known as "the Silver Seven," and they were the finest team in the land.

At least some of the 2,200 people who crowded into Ottawa's Dey's Arena thought the Nuggets might have a chance. Their teenage goalie, Albert Forrest, kept the game close, and Ottawa was only up 3-1 at half time. But the second half was rough – lots of fighting and stick work, and lots of Ottawa goals. The final score was 9-2 for Ottawa. Surprisingly, only one of Ottawa's goals was scored by McGee.

A member of the Dawson City team made the mistake of saying that McGee didn't look so hot. So, in the second game, McGee answered back with fourteen goals, eight of them in an eight-minute and twenty-second onslaught. It is a Stanley Cup record that still stands. The final score of the second game was 23-2.

The Nuggets went on a tour of the rest of the country before finally dispersing in Brandon, Manitoba. Albert Forrest made the 300-mile journey from Whitehorse to Dawson City by himself and on foot because there was no train, and he didn't have a bicycle.

CHAPTER TWO

Hockey's First Superstar

Opposite: Three of the greatest stars of early hockey pose in their Renfrew Millionaires sweaters in 1909-10. Renfrew, a small Ontario town, badly wanted to win the Stanley Cup. When the team purchased the talents of three of the game's great players, Edouard "Newsy" Lalonde (left), Frank Patrick (seated), and Fred "Cyclone" Taylor, they reckoned they were on their way. It was not to be. Lalonde went on to star with the Montreal Canadiens. Frank Patrick (with his brother Lester) started a league of his own. And Fred Taylor became hockey's first true superstar.

T

he prize was a new pair of $5 skates. In the winter of 1900, $5 was the weekly wage at the local piano factory. Fourteen-year-old Fred Taylor coveted those skates, and he knew a thing or two about skating. He regularly brought hockey-mad crowds to their feet in the new arena in the little town of Listowel in southern Ontario. To win the skates, all he had to do was beat an American speed skater in a quarter-mile race. And the American, Norval Baptie, would be skating backwards.

Baptie was born in Bethany, Ontario, but moved to North Dakota with his family as an infant. By the time he was ten he was winning skating races. And by the time he was twenty-one he had won so many races that he decided to make skating his profession. He traveled from town to town and dared the fastest skaters to beat him.

Baptie quickly took a thirty-foot head start against Fred Taylor, and before the two skaters had made two turns of the rink, Taylor had figured out just how he was going to lose. "Each time I'd get close enough to pass, he'd swing out just enough to block me off, just a little shift and a subtle move of the hips," he recalled. "Right away, I began to appreciate the art of skating backwards. The trick wasn't the speed but the balance and maneuverability. Right then and there, I told myself I was going to learn to become as good at it as he was."

Taylor took the lesson to heart. He became the fastest rushing defenseman in the game. Fans loved him. But when

13

The Kenora Thistles:
In 1907, the Kenora Thistles, led by Art Ross (front row, far right), won the Stanley Cup – the smallest town to ever do so. In the early days of Stanley Cup challenges, teams from towns of any size could compete for the Cup. As the game became professional, bigger towns became more powerful because they could afford the best players. Even so, the Thistles, from a town of 4,000 in northwestern Ontario, were too fast for the Montreal Wanderers, and won the two-game series in an upset. But winning the Cup in the early days of challenges didn't mean that a team could sit around and gloat. Two months later, they had to defend their title against another challenger. The Thistles traveled to Brandon, Manitoba – and won again.

he was just eighteen years old, Taylor thought his hockey career was over.

This was still the era of the amateur, when team owners could make money, but players could not. Players were supposed to play for the love of the game. Taylor loved hockey, but he couldn't afford to play for nothing. He needed his job in Listowel's piano factory. When the Toronto Marlboroughs offered him a place on the team, he said thanks, but no thanks. W.A. Hewitt, president of the Ontario Hockey Association, answered Taylor's refusal to play for Toronto by banning him from playing anywhere in Ontario.

Taylor sat out for a year and hated it. Then the town of Portage La Prairie in Manitoba – not much bigger than Listowel, but not in Ontario – offered him a place to play. This time, Taylor moved, and he quickly showed his stuff. He scored two goals against Winnipeg in his first game. In his next game,

The Guardian of Amateur Sport:
William A. Hewitt, a newspaper reporter and editor, became secretary to the Ontario Hockey Association in 1903. He kept the post for thirty years. He banned Cyclone Taylor from playing in the OHA. He managed the Winnipeg Falcons when the team won Olympic gold. And he was the father of Foster Hewitt, who became famous as the play-by-play announcer, first on radio and then on television, from Maple Leaf Gardens.

Right: After watching him score four spectacular goals for Ottawa on January 11, 1908, Earl Grey, Canada's governor-general, remarked that "Fred Taylor was a cyclone if ever I saw one." The nickname stuck.

he got a hat trick against the Rat Portage Thistles, supposedly the fastest team in hockey.

After the game, Thistles' stars Si Griffis and Tom Phillips waited for Taylor outside his dressing room. They invited him to join their team to challenge the mighty Montreal Wanderers for the Stanley Cup. Taylor couldn't believe it. A year ago he was out of hockey, and now he could be playing for the game's greatest prize.

But then he got another offer. This one was from John McNaughton, manager of the Portage Lakes team in Houghton, Michigan. McNaughton wanted him to play for his team – and for money. So instead of heading west to Manitoba, Fred Taylor headed south. There, for the princely sum of $400, he helped the Portage Lakes team beat their rivals in Pittsburgh for the championship of the International Hockey League – the world's first professional league.

Taylor had everything going for him. But there was just one problem: the pro teams couldn't challenge for the Stanley Cup and Taylor wanted a crack at the Jug. And he was a wanted man himself.

By 1907, Canadian teams had lost many of their best players to professional teams in the United States. At last, they gave up the idea that players had to be amateurs, and set out to lure stars such as Fred Taylor back home with offers of money.

Taylor decided to go to Ottawa, where he received $500 to play for the Senators. In 1909, the year he won his famous nickname, "Cyclone" Taylor led the Senators to their first Stanley Cup since the days of Frank McGee.

The following year Taylor moved to the Renfrew Creamery Kings, a team in a new pro league called the

National Hockey Association. The wealthy owners of the NHA badly wanted to win the Stanley Cup. They paid Taylor an astounding $5,200 for a twelve-game season.

In February 1910, Taylor made a famous boast. He was in the newsroom of the *Ottawa Citizen* when he told a reporter – in the presence of Ottawa goalie Percy Lesueur – that he would "skate through the Ottawa defense backward and score a goal."

Two days later, 7,000 Senators' fans – the largest crowd yet to witness a hockey game in Canada – came to hurl abuse, lemons, horse manure, and even empty whisky bottles at Cyclone Taylor. They were angry because their former favorite had betrayed them by following the money to Renfrew – and then insulted them with his taunt. Taylor, along with his defense partner, Lester Patrick, played a superb game, but he never got a shot on Ottawa's Percy Lesueur. Taylor was hooted out of town.

One month later, on March 8, 1910, the Cyclone tried again. The *Renfrew Mercury* reported that he skated down ice "in his usual fine fashion," and then "turned, going backwards, he skated a piece, and then sent the shot home to the Ottawa nets with skill and swiftness." Taylor's goal was backhanded, not backwards, but it was enough to launch the fable of Taylor's amazing "backwards goal."

For all the skill of its star player, and for all its money, the NHA still couldn't buy the Stanley Cup. However, two of the league's players, Frank and Lester Patrick, developed a different Cup strategy. They would move to British Columbia and start another league; the Pacific Coast League. They would build the

Left: At different times in his career, Fred Taylor was called a "wonder," a "whirlwind," and finally, a "cyclone." It was as Cyclone Taylor that he became famous as a goal-scoring wizard from Ottawa to New York to Vancouver. At one time, Taylor earned more money for his hockey genius than Prime Minister Wilfrid Laurier did for running Canada.

Montreal Star: Edouard "Newsy" Lalonde got his nickname when he worked as a printer's assistant at a newspaper. He starred in the first pro league in the United States, and was an original Montreal Canadien. He was traded to Renfrew, and on March 11, 1910, scored 11 goals in one game – a record that has never been beaten.

Stick Handler: Ernie "Moose" Johnson had the longest stick in hockey, and the longest reach: ninety-nine inches. (There was no regulation on stick length in hockey's early days.) After winning Stanley Cups with the Montreal Wanderers, Johnson headed west in 1911 to play in the new Pacific Coast League. He wore the colors of New Westminster, Portland, and Victoria's Cougars. It was while playing in Victoria that he won his nickname, "Moose." He later claimed that he was the first Moose in sports history.

Ernie 'Moose' Johnson
Reach 99 inches
Portland Hockey Team
1914-15

Photo by
Woodruff & Raymond

The Pacific Coast Association: Frank (right) and Lester Patrick (below left) were eastern Canada hockey stars with big ideas. In 1911, they convinced their father, who had made a fortune in the timber business, to start a hockey league. On Canada's West Coast. On artificial ice. But this was no mad scheme. The Patricks built the world's biggest rink in Vancouver. They added teams in Victoria and New Westminster, BC, Seattle, and Portland.

The Patricks were true hockey pioneers. Thanks to them – and especially to Frank – we also have the modern game. They invented the blue line, player substitutions, numbered jerseys, and the penalty shot. They allowed the crediting of assists, the forward pass, and goalies to fall down to make saves. And just for good measure, they established a playoff system. In all, they contributed twenty-two rule changes to the game.

Among the last of the changes they made was to abandon the "rover" position in 1922-23. It was for changes like these that Frank Patrick is called "the brains of modern hockey." His brains weren't enough to save the league, however: it folded after the 1923-24 season.

HOCKEY RULES

Adopted by the
Pacific Coast Hockey Assn.
and the Western Canada
Hockey League

TEAMS AND COLORS:

REGINA, Red, White and Blue.
SASKATOON, Garnet and Blue.
EDMONTON, Royal Blue and White.
CALGARY, Yellow Blue and Black.
VICTORIA, Blue and Gold.
VANCOUVER, Maroon and White.
SEATTLE, Red, White and Green.

In interleague games, if colors clash, slip-overs will be used on visiting team.

SEASON 1923-24

No26

LESTER PATRICK of Renfrew Club.

No21

JACK LAVIOLETTE of Canadian Club.

No2

PERCY LESUEUR of Ottawa Club.

31.

ARTHUR ROSS

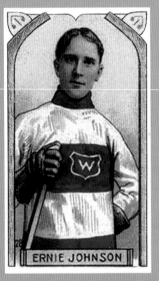

28

ERNIE JOHNSON

BERT LINDSAY

15

BRUCE STUART

25

ODIE CLEGHORN

24

SPRAGUE CLEGHORN

D. PITRE

E.D. LALONDE

J. LAVIOLETTE

Right: Coach and manager Frank Patrick (front, center) had the makings of a championship team in the 1913-14 Vancouver Millionaires of the Pacific Coast Hockey Association. Didier "Cannonball" Pitre (back row, far right) had the hardest shot of any player in his time. And Cyclone Taylor (front row, second from right) was known as the league's main goal-scoring threat. Pitre returned to Montreal the next season, but Taylor stayed and scored 23 goals in 16 games during the regular season and added 8 more in three playoff games to lead the Millionaires to their first and only Stanley Cup title.

Left: Hockey cards first appeared in 1910, when the British America Tobacco Company printed a color set of players from the National Hockey Association. The Imperial Tobacco Cigarettes collection included early hockey's greatest stars, including Art Ross of the Montreal Wanderers, Jack Laviolette of the Montreal Canadiens, Lester Patrick of Renfrew, and Percy Lesueur of Ottawa. By 1913, three different cigarette companies packed hockey cards with the cigarettes. They hoped to increase their sales by attracting hockey fans. Today, these same cards, if in mint condition, are worth thousands of dollars.

biggest artificial ice rink in the world in Vancouver, and another one in Victoria. They would put teams in those cities, plus New Westminster, and eventually, Seattle and Portland.

But there was one piece missing in the Patrick brothers' Stanley Cup dreams: Cyclone Taylor. So they offered Taylor a fat paycheque, and the Cyclone headed west. He played in an exhibition game that filled all 10,500 seats of Vancouver's new Denman Arena. And soon, he was the star of the Vancouver Millionaires, leading them to the city's first Stanley Cup in 1915. Frank Patrick, a hockey innovator of genius, knew that Taylor was in a class by himself. It was he who coined a special term for him: the Cyclone, he said, was hockey's first "superstar."

Blood and Ice

Sixty-six million soldiers and civilians died in the First World War. Frank Frederickson was almost one of them.

Frederickson's parents came to Canada from Iceland. They wanted him to be like other Canadian kids. Because the children in their Winnipeg neighborhood all played hockey, they bought their son skates and built him a backyard rink. Hockey then taught him how to speak English – he picked it up as he played. He became proficient at both the language and the game. So proficient, in fact, that he went on to be captain of the Winnipeg Falcons hockey team and led it to a Manitoba Hockey League championship in 1915. All but one of the players' families came originally from Iceland.

The next year, at the age of twenty-one, Frederickson enlisted in a battalion of the Canadian army made up mainly of university students from Western Canada. Because of his background, however, he was transferred, along with several of his Falcons teammates, to the 223rd Scandinavian Battalion.

Frederickson nearly died when his ship was torpedoed by a German submarine on the way to Egypt. A Japanese destroyer found him floating in a life raft in the Mediterranean Sea. He was wearing only pajamas and clutching his violin.

When Frederickson returned to Winnipeg in 1919, he wanted to play hockey again, and so did those of his old Falcons teammates who had also survived the war. But the Manitoba senior

Opposite: Frank Frederickson was born in Winnipeg in 1895 to parents who had emigrated from Iceland. He learned to speak English by playing hockey with the neighbors' children. He went on to play as an amateur, leading his team to the Olympics, and then he turned pro. He was playing for Victoria in the Pacific Coast League when his team won the Stanley Cup in 1925.

league wouldn't let them. Even though Frederickson and his friends had fought for Canada, some people still looked down on them as poor immigrants. "We found that the reason we couldn't get into the senior league was because the players were from well-to-do families and wanted no part of us," Frederickson said later. "But they couldn't quite get away from us that easily."

Frederickson approached the sports editor of the *Winnipeg Free Press* to help him form an independent hockey league. With the editor's encouragement, two other teams agreed to join them. The editor also convinced Fred "Steamer" Maxwell to be their coach. Maxwell had won his nickname because of his tremendous skating power. He refused to turn professional and quit the Winnipeg Monarchs in 1915 when he learned that some of the other players were taking money. He still held to the belief that people should play games for love, not cash.

The Falcons were rusty. They hadn't played for a few years. But "by the end of the season," Frederickson recalled, "Steamer had welded us into a great team. We whipped the Manitoba league champions and later the Lakehead winner to enter the Allan Cup against Toronto Varsity."

The Allan Cup was donated in 1908 by Sir Hugh Allan, a Montreal tycoon. The trophy was intended to be (and it still is) the top prize for senior men's amateur hockey in Canada. But more than Sir Hugh's trophy was at stake this time. The winner would go to Europe to play in the Olympic Games.

Most people reckoned that the Toronto team would easily beat the Winnipeg Falcons. More than 8,000 fans lined up to cheer them on. They were in for a surprise: Frederickson's team won easily.

The Icelanders had no time to return to Winnipeg after the series. Instead, they boarded a ship bound for Europe just as they had a few years earlier when they went to war. This time, though, their weapons were hockey sticks. The ship's carpenter made them new ones during the eight-day journey, from wood specially purchased in Montreal.

Above: Sir Hugh Allan, a wealthy Montreal industrialist, gave Canadian amateur hockey the Allan Cup in 1908. The Stanley Cup, by this time, was the prize for professional teams. The Allan Cup would be the prize for amateurs. When the Canadian Amateur Hockey Association was formed in 1914, the Allan Cup became its trophy, to be won by the best senior amateur men's hockey team in the country.

Below: When the Winnipeg Falcons were asked to represent Canada in the Olympic Games, they had no time before they boarded the ship to Europe to go home to get equipment. Each player was given $25 to buy new clothes. Extra sticks were made for them by the ship's carpenter. They wore their Canada sweaters proudly as they sailed to hockey glory.

Above: After they defeated the Toronto Varsity Grads to win the 1920 Allan Cup, the Winnipeg Falcons were asked to represent Canada in the 1920 Olympic Games. Their skilled, fast play delighted the Europeans and confounded their opponents, whom they outscored 29-1.

The 1920 Olympic Games were unusual for a couple of reasons. For one thing, the previous games had been canceled because of the war, so these were the first Olympic Games after a long pause. For another, these games would combine summer and winter sports. And it would be the first time ice hockey was part of any Olympic Games

Seven countries entered hockey teams: Canada, the United States, Switzerland, Belgium, Sweden, France, and Czechoslovakia. Attendance at the games was low – the war had made people poor. Hockey, however, was a game that everyone wanted to see. And the Canadians were dazzling, racking up goals with ease, and trying hard to be good sports.

The Europeans had suffered enormous losses – of both life and property – during the war. They appreciated the part Canada had played in defeating the German invaders and were more than willing to admire the Canadian team. So many people crowded outside the Palais de Glace to wait for the Falcons to arrive that the team had to be escorted to their dressing room by soldiers.

The confident American team wanted to wager some cash on the game. "One of the Americans was sure they'd beat us and offered a good sized bet," Frederickson said later. "Our treasurer never told us, but he took him up on that wager."

High Flyer: Hobart Amory Baker's hockey talents were so fine that he has been called hockey's first American superstar. He played rover, a free-flowing position in the old "seven man aside" game, for his university team, the Princeton Tigers. They played their home games in New York City's St. Nicholas Rink, which would advertise "Hobey Baker Plays Here Tonight" because he was so talented and famous. After graduation, Baker joined the St. Nicholas Rink's amateur hockey team. When Baker and St. Nick's played the Montreal Stars for the Ross Cup on December 11, 1915, Baker scored twice and set up three goals to lead St. Nick's to a 6-2 victory. Baker was offered $3,500 to come to Canada and turn pro, but he only played for love, and refused. Baker became a pilot in the First World War, and won the Croix de Guerre for his courage under fire. Shortly after the war ended, the 26-year-old Baker took an airplane up for a test flight and was killed when it crashed. He is remembered with the award bearing his name for the best US college hockey player.

The Canadians beat the United States 2-0, and the delighted treasurer presented each Falcon with a suit of new clothes purchased from his winnings. The head of the Canadian Olympic program found out and wanted to punish the team because the bet violated their amateur status. "He wanted to have us deprived of our title and medals for having accepted those gifts," Frederickson remembered, "but nothing happened."

Frederickson and his fellow Canadians defeated their opponents by a combined score of 29-1. The only goal they allowed was to Sweden. The Canadians thought Sweden to be the best of the European teams and "very friendly fellows . . . we liked them a lot." The fact that the Swedes were also Scandinavian helped, too. "I guess it's safe to confess that we gave it to them," said Frederickson later. "The Swedes went wild. They were yelling and cheering, shaking hands with themselves, shaking hands with us. It was great."

Five years later, the International Olympic Committee decided that the winter games would be "official" only from 1924 onward. Frederickson's gold medal no longer counted. But the Falcons had shown the world how good they were, and Canada had breezed to triumph in the first World Championship. In the years to come, Canadians would expect nothing less than total victory when it came to hockey.

The NHL Is Born: The National Hockey League came into existence because of a dispute among businessmen. The directors of the National Hockey Association met at Montreal's Windsor Hotel on November 6, 1917, because the league was in trouble. Quebec City's franchise had money problems. The Toronto club was owned by Eddie Livingstone and the other owners found him "difficult." The NHA owners came up with a simple solution. They would form a new league that would exclude Toronto. And then news arrived that Eddie Livingstone had sold his Toronto franchise. Suddenly, financially strapped Quebec offered to withdraw to make room for the Livingstone-free Toronto team – but only if they were allowed to sell their players for $700 a man. They were and did. Frank Calder (right) was elected president and secretary-treasurer of the "new" league. (The NHL rookie-of-the-year trophy is named after him.) In the hotel corridor after the meeting broke up, a young Montreal *Herald* sports reporter, Elmer Ferguson, rushed up to Calder and asked what had happened to professional hockey in Canada. "Not too much, Fergie," Calder replied. And so the National Hockey League was born.

The Preston Rivulettes: Hilda (above) and Nellie Ranscombe were star baseball players on a local women's softball team. At the end of the 1930 baseball season, they wanted to keep their team together throughout the winter, so they decided to play hockey. A neighborhood boy laughed at them, saying that girls couldn't play hockey. It was all the women needed to hear. With Nellie in goal, and sister Hilda at right wing, and with the offensive gifts of the Schmuck sisters, Marm and Helen, the Preston Rivulettes were unstoppable. From 1930 to 1939, they won ten championship titles in both Ontario and Quebec, as well as six national champion titles. Their most amazing statistic is their record: just two losses and three ties in 350 games. When the Second World War began, travel restrictions and gas rationing made it hard for the Rivulettes to get to games, and they retired as the greatest women's hockey team of all time.

Canada's Team

In the autumn of 1906, when Constantine Falkland Cary Smythe was just eleven years old, his mother Mary died of complications due to alcoholism. "Constantine" was his mother's maiden name, but he thought it wasn't manly enough. So, when someone pointed out that he had never been baptized, he saw his chance, and as he always would, he took it. He decided that he would be known as Conn. It was a solid and fearless name, and he would do it proud.

Conn Smythe was always the smallest kid wherever he found himself – at school, on a hockey team, at war – but he always made up for it with a huge will and even bigger ambition. He was also a great patriot, and proudly wore the maple leaf when he signed up to serve as an artillery lieutenant in the First World War.

He subsequently got himself transferred from the ground and into the air as pilot of an artillery observation plane. He flew a type of aircraft nicknamed "the Incinerator" because it had the bad habit of bursting into flames on its own. So perhaps it wasn't surprising that Toronto newspapers reported Lieutenant Conn Smythe as "missing in action" in November 1917.

But Smythe was lucky. He was missing, but he was alive. He had been shot down and captured by the Germans. He almost got himself killed again when he put up a fight with the soldier who took him prisoner. The German shot Smythe twice from point-blank range. Smythe's thick, flying coat saved his life.

Opposite: Conn Smythe was a hockey player, coach, team manager, and then founder and owner of the Toronto Maple Leafs. He guided his team to seven Stanley Cups before his retirement in 1961.

When Smythe came home to Canada at the end of the war, he was twenty-four years old, and as he wrote later, "four years of my life were gone that I would never get back…. But I was going to make up for it, of that I was damn sure."

Smythe kept his promise. Before the war he had been a University of Toronto hockey player and coach. He got back into the game again, while running a gravel business and raising a young family with his wife, Irene.

He was a hockey man to the core of his being. When the NHL wanted to put another team in New York City, the New York Rangers turned to Conn Smythe. Smythe used his knowledge and smarts to recruit players that no one else seemed to know about. And that was a problem for the Rangers' owners. They looked at Smythe's roster and figured he had hired a team of nobodies. So they fired Smythe and refused for a time to pay him a quarter of the $10,000 that they owed him.

When Smythe finally got paid, he set out to get his revenge. He took the money – $2,500 – and bet it on a college football game between the University of Toronto and McGill. Toronto won and Smythe doubled his money. That night, the Toronto St. Pats hockey club was playing the New York Rangers. Because the Rangers were a new, untested team most people dismissed them, but Smythe was laughing. He had built the Rangers and he knew how good they were. So he bet on the Rangers, won, and then he had $10,000.

Smythe found other investors to help him buy the Toronto St. Pats. He took them out of their green-and-white uniforms,

Chicoutimi Cuke: Georges Vezina was playing for Chicoutimi when he shut out the mighty Canadiens. They promptly signed him and he started in net for Montreal in the 1910-11 season. He was called the "Chicoutimi Cucumber" for his cool style under fire. He never missed a regular season or playoff game during his fifteen years with Montreal. They won five Stanley Cups with him in net. But on the night of November 28, 1925, he had to leave the game when he started bleeding from the mouth. Four months later he was dead of tuberculosis. The Canadiens donated a trophy in his name, which has come to honor the NHL's best goaltender each season.

Right: Francis "King" Clancy came to the Maple Leafs from Ottawa on October 11, 1930. Clancy was the final ingredient owner Conn Smythe needed in his quest to win the Stanley Cup.

and put them in the blue-and-white of his beloved university. Then – always the patriot – he renamed them the Maple Leafs. And Smythe made a bold promise. Within five years, he said, his Maple Leafs would win the Stanley Cup. The year was 1927.

Once again, Smythe turned to gambling to help make his dream come true. "Most people think of 1930 as the first year of the Depression," he said. "I think of it as the year we got King Clancy."

When the stock market crashed in 1929, many people lost their jobs, their homes, and some, their lives. Times were hard and money was scarce. Professional hockey offered an escape from troubled times, but even with a top-notch team, Smythe wasn't filling the seats in Toronto's old Mutual Street Arena. He needed a star player. He needed Francis "King" Clancy.

Below: The 1928-29 Toronto Maple Leafs stand outside their home rink, the Mutual Street Arena. In the center of the photo is goalie Lorne Chabot. Chabot had been playing for the Rangers when he was hit in the eye by a puck and the Rangers' management thought he went soft. Conn Smythe didn't think so and brought him to Toronto. In his first season, Chabot posted a stingy 1.61 goals-against average and had twelve shutouts in forty-three games.

Cowboy on Ice: Alec Antoine was the star player with the Alkali Lake Braves, a team of aboriginal players from the Cariboo ranching country of British Columbia. With stocky, powerful Antoine at center, the Braves were a fine team, and in 1931 they defeated Prince George to win the Northern BC league title. As a result, they received an offer in January 1932, to play in Vancouver. The Braves played only about eight games a season on outdoor rinks. Now they found themselves in an artificial ice rink holding 4,000 fans, playing against an all-star team from the big city. Back home in the Cariboo, people tuned in to their radios to listen to the matches. Despite predictions that they would be slaughtered, the Braves held their own, losing both matches by just one goal. Lester Patrick was so impressed by Alec Antoine that he offered him a job in the NHL with the New York Rangers, but Antoine said he already had a job, as a cowboy earning $15 a week. So he went home to his Alkali Lake Ranch.

Clancy had broken into the NHL in 1921 when he was seventeen. He was one of the smallest pro-defensemen to play the game, just five-foot-seven and 155 pounds. He was small, but fearless, and never backed away from a fight. Clancy was just the type of man Smythe wanted on his team.

The Senators wanted $35,000 for him, but Smythe had only $25,000. So once again, Conn Smythe made a bet.

He owned a race horse, Rare Jewel, that had never won a race. The odds against her winning in the "Coronation Futurity" race were huge: 200-1. This meant that no one in their right mind thought Rare Jewel had a hope of winning. Smythe bet $60 on his horse, and when she won her first and only race, he found himself about $11,000 richer. To this he added the $3,750 he received as owner of the winning horse. He had more than enough to buy the "King."

Now that he had his star, Smythe decided he needed a grander arena. He convinced Eaton's department store to sell him a parcel of land at the corner of Church and Carlton streets in exchange for $350,000 and an option to buy shares in the new arena. When money ran short, Smythe's lieutenant, Frank Selke, convinced the trade unions building the arena to take payment in shares, too.

On June 1, 1931, work began on Maple Leaf Gardens. Just five months later, it was finished. On November 12, 1931, army

Above: Workers started construction of a new arena for the Maple Leafs on June 1, 1931. Less than six months later, Maple Leaf Gardens opened, while bands from the Royal Grenadiers and the 48th Highlanders played "Happy Days Are Here Again" to an audience of 13,000.

One, Two, Three . . . Again!: The Toronto Maple Leafs work out in the 1930s. Dry-land training was unusual for a hockey team in those days. It wasn't until decades later that all teams began to use comprehensive fitness training.

The Man Wearing the Cap: He was nicknamed the "Little Giant" as a joke, because he stood just five-foot-six, and weighed less than 140 pounds, but Aurele Joliat's hockey talent was huge. He played left wing to Howie Morenz's center and the duo led the Montreal Canadiens to two straight Stanley Cups in 1930 and 1931. He was fast and slippery, and he could put the puck in the net – he scored 270 NHL goals, the same number as the great Morenz.

"The Stratford Streak": He was one of the greatest hockey players ever, but when he signed up to play with the Montreal Canadiens in 1923, he had second thoughts. Howie Morenz was a big star in his hometown of Stratford, and he was afraid he might not be able to make it in the NHL. He even sent back his signing bonus of $850 on a contract of $2500 a year. The Canadiens would have none of it. They told Morenz that if he didn't play for them, he wouldn't play for anyone. Morenz played his first shift with Montreal on Boxing Day, 1923, in Ottawa's new rink. Before a record crowd of 8,300 fans, Morenz scored the first of the 270 goals that he would tally in the NHL. After beating Vancouver, champs of the Pacific Coast Association, Morenz and the Canadiens took on the Calgary Tigers for the 1924 Stanley Cup championship. Morenz was on a blazingly fast line with the "Little Giant" Aurele Joliat on one wing, and Billy Boucher on the other. He came first in scoring with seven goals in the playoffs and a Stanley Cup victory. Morenz was so talented that when the builder of New York's new Madison Square Garden arena saw him play, he agreed to put ice – and hockey – in his building.

Morenz broke his leg during a game against Chicago in January, 1937, and he knew his career was over. On March 8, he suffered a coronary embolism in hospital, and died. He was just thirty-four. Fifty thousand people walked past his casket in the Montreal Forum. And a quarter of a million more lined the route to the cemetery to say good-bye.

Above: Foster Hewitt became famous to generations of Canadians as the play-by-play voice of the Toronto Maple Leafs. He called his first game on February 16, 1923, as a twenty-three-year-old sports reporter seated in a rinkside box at the Mutual Street Arena. It was so cramped that his breath made the glass in front of him foggy. To make matters worse, he had to call the game over the telephone. Phone operators kept interrupting him to ask what number he was calling.

Caged Lightning: Canadian hockey players looking for work during the tough years of the Depression often turned to Europe. The Français Volants (Flying Frenchmen), a hockey team based in Paris from 1933 to 35, were almost entirely Quebecois. Their captain, Roger Gaudette, was described in a British hockey program as "caged lightning with a burst of speed that puts him with the speediest puckchasers in Europe." Gaudette recalled that playing in Europe often posed difficulties when it came to travel. "We played everywhere, in the great capital cities: Prague, Vienna, Budapest, Berlin, London and Paris. We played twenty-four games a season, running from one place to the other. It wasn't always easy! We'd often attract crowds of 20,000 spectators."

bands played "Happy Days Are Here Again" to an opening night audience of more than 13,000 fans.

Foster Hewitt, who would become famous as hockey's greatest play-by-play radio announcer, began his broadcast of the game with his trademark, "Hello, Canada, the United States, and Newfoundland." He was perched on a tiny platform hanging from the rafters – one that would also become famous as the romantically named "gondola."

The Leafs lost their first game in Maple Leaf Gardens to the Chicago Black Hawks. But they had a good season and met the New York Rangers – the team Smythe had built – in the Stanley Cup finals. The Leafs won the best-of-five game series in three, straight games; the last one at home in front of their overjoyed fans. Conn Smythe had kept the promise made five years earlier: the Leafs had won the Stanley Cup. Canada's team was on its way.

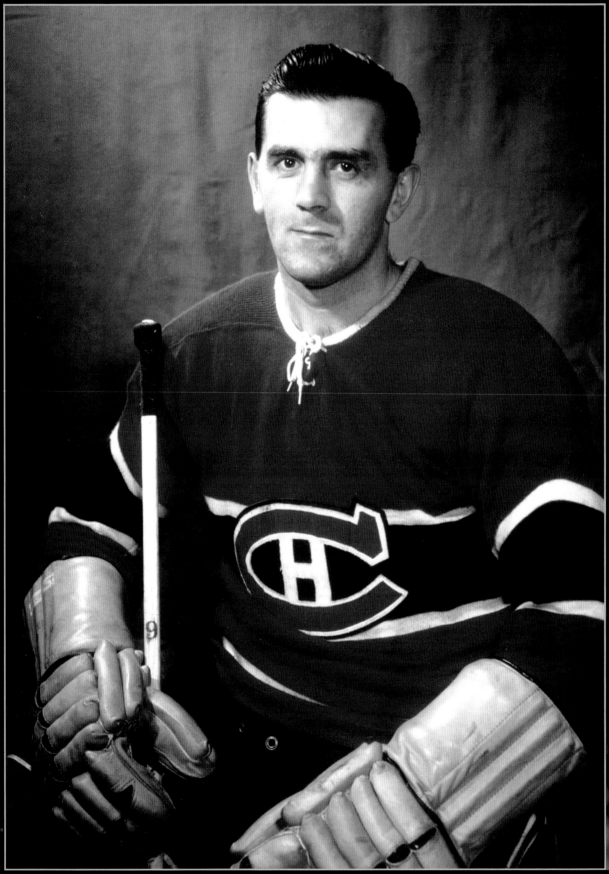

CHAPTER FIVE

The Rocket's Red Glare

While large parts of English Canada cheered for the Toronto Maple Leafs during the 1940s, in Quebec the Montreal Canadiens were the "national" team, and their greatest star was Maurice "Rocket" Richard. Richard was more than a hockey player. His talent, his passion, and his refusal to bend to authority made him, in the words of one writer, "a flag for a people."

Richard's skill was obvious from an early age, but a number of observers doubted that he would last for long in the NHL. He was cursed, they said, with brittle bones.

In 1940, Richard tried out with a senior team owned by the Canadiens. He scored two goals in his first game, and then, in that same game, he caught his skate in a rut and broke his left ankle. The following year he broke his wrist. And then, in his first season with the Canadiens (1942-43), he broke his right ankle. Even his coach in Montreal, Dick Irvin, worried that Richard was too fragile.

Perhaps his bones did break easily, but Richard's will to win was superhuman. When he had the puck on his stick and was racing in on goal, his dark eyes were like lasers, and goalies were scared of him. When his second ankle injury healed, Irvin teamed him up with silky center Elmer Lach, and left-winger Hector "Toe" Blake. Together, the trio became known as "The Punch Line."

In the second game of the 1944 Stanley Cup semifinals against the Toronto Maple Leafs, the Rocket showed his awesome power

Opposite: Maurice Richard was called the "Rocket" because of the way he rocketed in on goalies. He was the first NHL player to score 50 goals in a season, and the first to score 500 in his career. A generation of people in Quebec saw him as the man who lived out their dreams of greatness on ice.

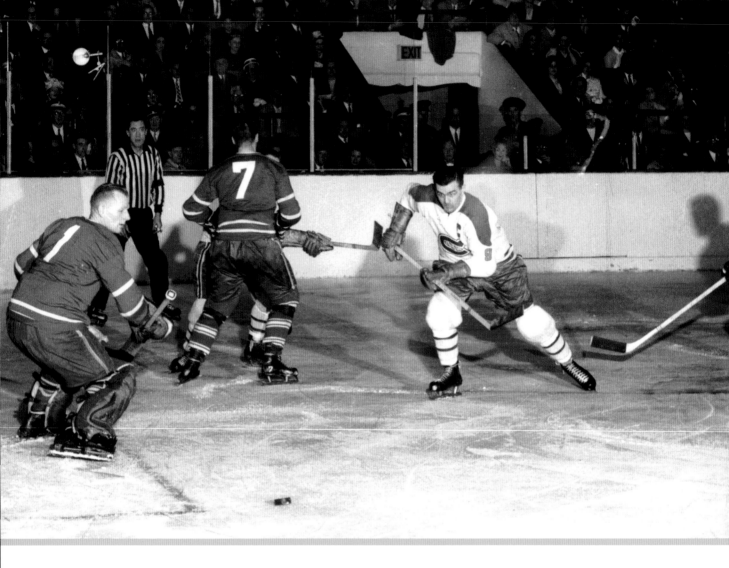

by scoring his first two goals just seventeen seconds apart in the first two minutes of the game. He made it a natural hat trick before the period was out. Then, in the third period, he scored twice more to tie Newsy Lalonde's record of five Stanley Cup goals in one game. With the final score Maple Leafs 1, Rocket Richard 5, there was only one thing left to do: Richard was named all three of the game's three stars.

Three days after Christmas 1944, Richard moved into a new house. He didn't supervise the movers: he shifted the furniture, including a piano, himself. It was a game day and Richard arrived in the Montreal dressing room seemingly exhausted. He lay down on the training table as if to send a message to his teammates not to count on him that night.

But the Rocket was just taking a breather. When the time came, he unleashed his ferocious powers, scoring five goals and

Above: Toronto goalie Johnny Bower watches Richard hunt down a loose puck in the 1960 Stanley Cup final against the Maple Leafs. The Canadiens swept the Leafs in four games to win their fifth straight Stanley Cup. It was Rocket Richard's last Cup: he retired at the start of the next season.

A Girl in a Boy's League: In 1955, eight-year-old Abigail Hoffman (pictured above with Toronto Maple Leafs, Brian Cullen and Jim Morrison) registered for a new hockey league in Toronto – even though the organizers intended it to be for boys only. No one noticed that her birth certificate showed clearly that Abigail was a girl. She cut her hair short and called herself "Ab" to encourage the illusion. For three months, Ab Hoffman wore her gear to the rink like the other players. She became a stand-out on defense on the St. Catharine's, Ontario, Tee-Pees. She was even selected from among 400 players in the league to play on an all-star team. Then the news broke that she was really a girl. She became an instant celebrity in Canada and the United States – but the league wouldn't let her play anymore. She was forced to retire from her team at the age of nine.

Abigail went on to have a great athletic career in track and field. Her pioneering on ice led to the creation of girls' hockey leagues. Today, the Abby Hoffman Cup is awarded to the national champions of Canadian women's hockey.

picking up three assists in an eventual 9-1 rout of the Detroit Red Wings. In a nine-game stretch Richard fired in fourteen goals. He managed these heroics in spite of the lengths to which his opponents went in trying to stop him. They slashed, tripped, elbowed, hooked, and, when all that failed, hung on to him as if to tackle him.

Richard just shoved them away. If they kept bothering him, he could level them with a punch as powerful as that of any heavyweight boxer. He had to look after himself. In those days there were no "enforcers" around to fight his battles for him.

But there was one battle that consumed Richard more than anything else. He wanted to become the first man to score 50 goals in 50 games. When he beat ex-Canadien Joe Malone's record of 45 goals (set in 1918, over 22 games), he could taste the sweetness of victory. He still had eight games to reach the magical 50-in-50 that no one else had ever posted. But then, inexplicably, he got stuck at 49. No one wanted to be remembered for giving up that fiftieth goal.

It was the last period of the Canadiens' last home game and the stage was set for a perfect ending. Richard was alone in front of the Chicago net when a Black Hawk defenseman chopped him to the ice. And the referee gave Richard a penalty shot.

Here, surely, was number 50. It was like an old-fashioned duel. Richard, the hero, skated in alone against the Chicago goalie, the villain, and the crowd was on its feet, cheering him to glory. But it was not to be. The Chicago goalie stopped him cold. And now things were really tense, for Richard had just one game left to make his dream come true.

Would he do it? Could he do it? It was late in the third period of the final game of the season, in a hostile Boston Garden, and Richard still hadn't scored. Time was running out. And then suddenly, the Rocket scooped up a pass from Elmer Lach, and bang! Just like that, he fired it into Boston's net. And just in case anyone thought he got lucky, Richard added six more goals in six playoff games against the Maple Leafs and Black Hawks, making it an astonishing 56 goals in 56 games.

Richard is remembered for the passions he aroused off the ice as well as on it. In 1955, he was suspended from the playoffs after he struck a linesman during a fight. Fans were outraged.

Number 9: Gordie Howe (pictured above battling Leaf Larry Hillman for the puck during the 1960-61 season) started his NHL career at right-wing for the Red Wings in 1946. He scored in his first game. He was wearing sweater number 17 that year, and only changed to the famous number 9 the next year. Howe went on to play for an astonishing 26 seasons in the NHL plus 6 seasons in the WHA, and finished among the top 5 of NHL scorers for 20 straight seasons. When he was with Detroit, he was put on a line with Sid Abel and Ted Lindsay, and the three of them burned up the league as "The Production Line." Howe nearly lost his life in a 1950 playoff game against Toronto when he crashed hard into the boards, headfirst, and suffered a fractured skull. Howe, big and strong at six feet and two hundred pounds, made an amazing recovery. His long career was filled with triumphs. He was named an All-Star 21 times; he won the Art Ross Trophy six times as the NHL's top scorer; he won the Hart Trophy six times as the league's most valuable player; and he won the Stanley Cup four times with Detroit.

Boston Breakthrough: On January 18, 1958, Willie O'Ree became the first black player in NHL history when he took to the ice for Boston against Montreal. O'Ree only played two games for the Bruins that season, but in 1960-61 he caught on with the Bruins and played in 43 games, scoring four goals and notching ten assists. O'Ree was also playing with only one good eye – he had been hit in his right eye with a puck in 1956 and lost 95 percent of his vision in that eye. If the NHL had known about his semi-blindness, he would never have been allowed to play in the league at all.

Hockey Night in Canada: In 1952, the Canadian Broadcasting Corporation began transmitting television signals in Canada, first from Montreal on September 6, and then from Toronto on September 8. One month later, on October 11, 1952, Gerald Renaud, a twenty-four-year-old newspaper editor helped the new network put a hockey game between Montreal and Detroit on the air. On November 1, the CBC broadcast a game from Toronto, and Hockey Night in Canada/La Soirée du Hockey was born. For the first time, Canadian kids and their families who, before this, could only hear hockey broadcasts on the radio, now could see their favorite players and teams in action without leaving home. Saturday night would never be the same.

They believed their French-Canadian hero was the victim of English-Canadian injustice. They took to the streets of Montreal, where they overturned vehicles and trashed storefronts, in what became known as the Richard Riot.

Richard would top the goal-scoring chart five times in his long NHL career. He made the All-Star team fourteen consecutive times between 1944 and 1957. He was the first player to break the 500-career goal barrier, finishing with 544 regular season goals in 1960, the year of his last of eight Stanley Cup victories. He was then thirty-nine years old, and time and injuries had taken their toll. So Richard retired from the arena of hockey and stepped into that of legend, a true Canadian hero.

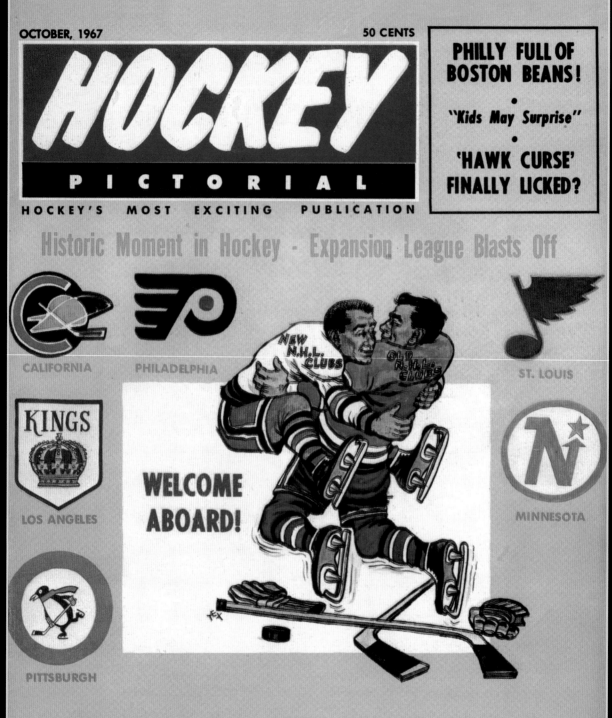

The National Birthday Party

It was the biggest birthday party in the country's history. It was 1967 and Canada was turning 100 years old. To celebrate, Montreal, Canada's then-largest and most cosmopolitan city, was hosting Expo 67, a fabulous world's fair. Fans of the Canadiens would have liked nothing better than to display the Stanley Cup to admiring crowds at Expo. But first, of course, they had to win it.

The year would be significant for the NHL as well. The Stanley Cup finals in 1967 marked the end of the era of the so-called "Original Six." For more than twenty years following the end of the Second World War, there were just six NHL teams: Toronto and Montreal in Canada; Detroit, Chicago, Boston, and New York in the United States. In the autumn of 1967, the NHL would double in size, adding six new teams in the United States. The league would be split up into a western and eastern division, and the winners of each would compete for the Stanley Cup.

Because both Montreal and Toronto were in the east, their great Cup rivalry was coming to an end, at least until the NHL expanded and rejigged the divisions again (which it did in 1981-82).

The sense of national drama was intense: a rivalry that had been one of the greatest in professional sports for nearly four decades was now reaching its glorious climax in the middle of the national birthday party. And both Toronto and Montreal thought that they deserved the Stanley Cup.

Opposite: At the beginning of the 1967 season, the NHL had the biggest growth spurt in its history. The league doubled its size by adding six "expansion" teams in Philadelphia, Pittsburgh, St. Louis, Minnesota, Oakland, and Los Angeles. To accommodate this growth, the league was divided into two divisions, with all of the expansion clubs residing in the West division, and the original six teams in the East. In 1974, the Philadelphia Flyers became the first expansion team to win the Stanley Cup.

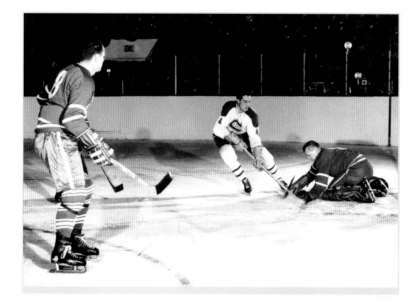

Left: In 1953, the Montreal Canadiens bought the entire Quebec Senior League and turned it pro just so they could sign the Quebec Aces' star center Jean Béliveau. Béliveau (shown trying to score on Johnny Bower while Larry Regan looks on) would play eighteen full seasons with the Canadiens, ten of them as their captain. His elegance both on and off the ice earned him great respect. His hockey talent won him the Art Ross Trophy as league scoring champ, and the Hart Trophy as most valuable player.

The two franchises had two dozen Cups between them. The Maple Leafs had been to the Stanley Cup final eighteen times, and had won the Jug on ten occasions. The Canadiens were nearly twenty years older as a franchise than the Leafs. They had won it fourteen times in twenty-three final appearances.

In April 1967, the Montreal Canadiens were favored to win the Cup again. They had talent in spades, with speedy Yvan "Roadrunner" Cournoyer and Rocket Richard's younger brother Henri "Pocket Rocket" Richard scoring nearly a fifth of the Canadiens 536 regular season points. They were led by their elegant, playmaking captain Jean Béliveau, and with tough guy John Ferguson in the lineup, they weren't going to let their talent get pushed around.

The Leafs, older than the Canadiens, were jokingly nicknamed the "Over-the-Hill Gang." Defensemen Marcel Pronovost was 36, Tim Horton was 37, and Allan Stanley was 41. Center Red Kelly was 39, while goalies Terry Sawchuk and Johnny Bower were 37 and 42 respectively. Their 36-year-old captain George Armstrong was the last of nine Leaf captains personally selected by Conn Smythe. Armstrong was affectionately nicknamed the "Chief," partly because of his Iroquois mother, and partly because Alberta's Stoney Indian tribe had given him the honorary title, "Big-Chief-Shoot-the-Puck." Armstrong could score too: He amassed a total of 713 points in 1187 regular season NHL games.

Unsung Hero: Toronto Maple Leafs equipment manager Tommy Naylor checks out the blade of a skate. Naylor invented the goalie's trapper and blocker, created body armor, made improvements to the skate boot and blade, and built the world's first portable skate sharpener. Executives from hockey equipment companies showed up at his workshop in Maple Leaf Gardens regularly and "borrowed" his ideas, for which he never received a cent.

It looked as if the Leafs might be the "Too-Far-Over-the-Hill Gang" when the Canadiens easily won the first game 6-2. But then the Leafs came back in the second game when the old guy, Bower, shut out the Canadiens 3-0. The third game was a goalies' battle, too. Montreal's young Rogie Vachon stopped 62 shots, and Bower stopped 54, before Bob Pulford won it for Toronto eight nail-biting minutes into the second overtime period.

Game four was played on the opening day of Expo '67, and bad luck struck the Leafs early when Johnny Bower injured his groin in the pre-game warm-up. So Terry Sawchuk went in net for the Leafs and had a bad game. After Sawchuk let six pucks get past him in a 6-2 Canadiens' victory, a fan sent him a telegram asking, "How much did you get?"

Sawchuk was as sensitive as he was tough. He was deeply wounded by the fan's accusation that he would take a bribe. He came back in Game five with the kind of goaltending genius that had made him a four-time Vezina winner, giving Toronto a 4-1 win over Montreal. The Over-the-Hill-Gang went home needing just one win to capture the prize.

Below: Leafs' captain George Armstrong duels with Montreal defenseman Jacques Laperriere in front of Canadiens' goalie Charlie Hodge during the 1966-67 season. The NHL's only two Canadian teams would meet in the Stanley Cup final – the best birthday present Canada could have as it celebrated its centennial in 1967.

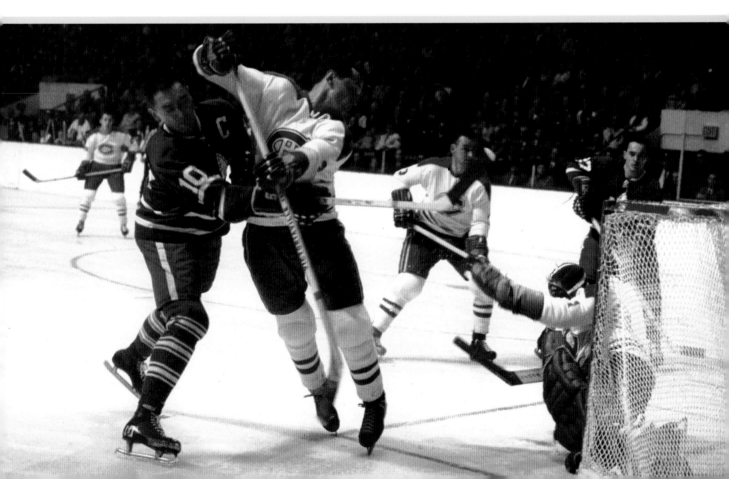

The Flying Fathers: Les Costello, a speedy, talented left-winger, won two Memorial Cups with Toronto's St. Michael's junior team and the 1948 Stanley Cup with the Maple Leafs. Then he heard the call to play for a different team and he left hockey to become a Roman Catholic priest. But hockey called him back. A fellow priest, Father Brian McKee, formed a team of hockey-playing priests in 1962 to raise money for a sick child in his parish. The antics of "The Flying Fathers" caught the imagination of the country and the world. Millions of spectators took delight in watching the comic priests take on local teams in charity games played across the continent. Costello's wit was apparent off the ice as well. During a meeting at the Vatican with Pope Paul VI, Costello noticed the Pope was holding a hockey stick upside down, and showed him the right way, in case people would think he was "trying to stir spaghetti." The Flying Fathers have raised more than $4 million for charity. Now in their fourth decade they have become a true hockey dynasty, with nearly 1,000 victories, and just a handful of losses. Their success, said Costello, is simple: "We win a lot of games because we cheat a lot."

George Armstrong and Allan Stanley felt confident of the Leafs' chances. They reckoned that if the old boys could survive coach "Punch" Imlach's brutal regular season practices, they could survive to win the series with Montreal.

Game six was played in Toronto on Tuesday, May 2. And, to the surprise of many, with less than a minute left in the game, the Leafs *were* winning, with a tight 2-1 lead. The desperate Canadiens pulled their goalie Gump Worsley to send out an extra man for a face-off in the Toronto zone. It was one of those heart-thumping hockey moments: everything would change if only the Canadiens won the face-off and scored.

On the Toronto bench, defenseman Allan Stanley listened as Imlach named the players who would be on the ice for this critical face-off. "Kelly, Armstrong, Pulford, Horton," said Imlach. Finally, he said "Stanley."

"I got one foot out of the gate," recalled Stanley, "and he says, 'You take the face-off.'" The crafty Imlach had a trick up his sleeve. The league had recently introduced a new interference rule. Before the rule change, defensemen taking the face-off would use their often superior size to push their opponent off the puck instead of winning the puck cleanly with their sticks. Imlach was counting on Stanley to find a way to do precisely what the new rule forbade.

Straight Shooter: One day in the mid-1960s, Chicago Black Hawk right-winger Stan Mikita (above) cracked the blade of his stick. It didn't snap off cleanly, so Mikita fired a puck at the boards in an attempt to break it – and instead invented the curved stick. Until then, players had used a straight stick blade, but when they saw how the puck curved and dipped unpredictably off a bent blade, hockey players everywhere adopted the new model.

The Eccentric Netminder: Jacques Plante was a terrific goalie and an original thinker who took up knitting to keep himself occupied between games. Probably it needed someone like him to change the way goalies faced the opposition.

For more than twenty-five years, goalies stopped flying pucks while leaving their faces unprotected. Montreal Maroons' goalie Clint Benedict was the first professional to wear a mask in 1930 after his nose was broken by a Howie Morenz blast from twenty-five feet out. Benedict's mask was a crude leather protector that hugged the face. Another quarter century passed. Then Plante, in the Canadiens' net, took another puck to the face and he decided that he had had enough. Plante, who played recreational baseball as a back-catcher, mentioned in a TV interview that he'd be interested in trying out any masks suitable for hockey goaltenders. A man in Granby, Quebec, sent him a plastic model that Plante used in practise for three years. Then another inventor sent him a better mask. Plante's coach was reluctant to let him wear it during games. The coach thought the mask would make his goalie feel too safe – and less sharp. All of that changed in a game against the New York Rangers at Madison Square Garden on November 1, 1959, when Plante's face was on the receiving end of an Andy Bathgate slapshot. Plante refused to go back into the game unless he was protected. His coach finally agreed to let him wear a mask and Montreal went on an eleven-game, unbeaten streak. The goalie mask was here to stay.

Father Bauer's Vision: Father David Bauer was the younger brother of a professional hockey player – Bobby Bauer played on Boston's famous "Kraut Line" with Milt Schmidt and Woody Dumart. Young David might have played in the NHL, too: he was a member of the Memorial Cup-winning Oshawa Generals team in 1944. But he stunned the hockey world when he decided to become a Roman Catholic priest instead. After his ordination in 1953, Father Bauer took up a teaching post at Toronto's St. Michael's College School. He coached the St. Michael's team to a Memorial Cup in 1961. But Bauer had a vision of a national team, where players would go to university and play hockey for their country. It was a noble idea. Bauer's national team won a bronze medal at the Winter Olympic Games held in Grenoble, France, in 1968. Although they never won gold, Father Bauer's teams did produce athletic and well-educated Canadian hockey players.

Blue-Line Genius: In 1960, scouts for the Boston Bruins were watching 14-year-old players at a Bantam hockey tournament when they noticed a five-foot-two, 110-pound, 12-year-old Pee Wee who was clearly the best player on the ice. His name was Robert Orr, and Boston wanted him very badly. He was going to become "the franchise player" who would bring glory to an organization that hadn't won the Stanley Cup since 1941. Orr was an aggressive defenseman who could take an opponent out with his body, or, if necessary, with his fist. But he was much more than that. He was also an offensive genius who changed the tempo of the game with his end-to-end rushes. Teams had to find new ways to defend against Bobby Orr.

Orr became the only defenseman ever to win the Art Ross Trophy twice as the NHL's leading scorer. In 1970, he scored the Stanley Cup-winning goal for Boston, and ended their twenty-nine-year drought. He won the Conn Smythe Trophy as the playoffs' most valuable player. He won it again in 1972, when he again scored the Stanley Cup-winning goal. Orr won the Norris Trophy an amazing eight straight times as the NHL's best defenseman. He would have won it more but for a series of crippling knee injuries that forced him to retire in his prime, when he was just thirty years old.

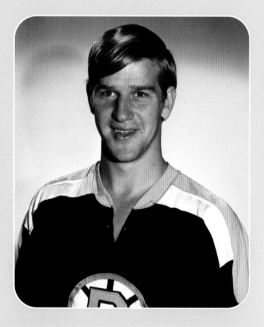

Right: Leaf captain George Armstrong holds the Stanley Cup aloft after the Leafs' victory over Montreal in 1967. Armstrong, who was part aboriginal, was "the best captain the Leafs ever had" according to team founder Conn Smythe, a tough judge of character.

He did. Stanley won the draw and shoveled the puck behind him where Red Kelly would retrieve it, then stepped into Jean Béliveau to block him. "He was the most surprised guy in the world," said Stanley. Kelly passed to Pulford, who passed to George Armstrong, who had a clear shot at an open net. "And while this is going on," said Stanley, "Jean was yelling to the ref, 'Face-off interference! Face-off interference!' But no referee in the world is going to make a call like that at a time like that."

And then it was over: Armstrong scored into an empty net. The Leafs had won their eleventh Stanley Cup. The Over-the-Hill Gang was on top of the world as the 48th Highlanders pipe band led their championship parade to Toronto's new city hall. But even though there was obvious disappointment in Montreal, the Stanley Cup series had pitted Canada's two great teams in an epic battle that reminded all Canadians that hockey was at the heart of the country's idea of itself.

The idea soon would be tested on an international stage. But for now, Canada reveled in the glorious summer of its hundredth year.

CHAPTER SEVEN

Us & Them

Paul Henderson wasn't a superstar. He was a solid, hard-working Toronto Maple Leaf who, in 1972, had just come off his best NHL season. The curly haired left-winger knew his way to the net and would fight hard to get there. That's why he was picked to play for Team Canada in the most important hockey contest in the history of the country.

For years, Canada had been sending amateur teams to world tournaments. Canadian fans always believed that, if only they could send their best professional players, they would show that they were the best in the world. In the 1960s, Canada developed a national team. But John "Bunny" Ahearne, the powerful president of the International Ice Hockey Federation, still would not allow Canada to fill it with NHL players. Frustrated hockey fans across Canada could only continue to mutter, *We could beat the Russians if only we could send our best!*

At last, in the summer of 1972, Canada got its chance. Prime Minister Pierre Trudeau was on a state visit to the USSR when he proposed to his hosts that the two countries face off in a series of hockey games. At the time, the USSR was a Communist superpower, and the enemy of western democracy in the Cold War. But the Soviets were interested in the idea. They, too, loved hockey, and they, too, thought they were the best.

Paul Henderson, a solid twenty-nine-year-old left winger with the Toronto Maple Leafs, was one of the last players selected for Team Canada. He responded by scoring the game-winning goal in the last three "must-win" games for Canada and became a hero to the entire country.

Opposite: Team Canada's Phil Esposito fights off Soviet defenseman Alexander Gusev to get to the puck during the historic 1972 Summit Series. "Espo" was the series scoring leader with thirteen points.

Team Canada and the USSR squad prepare to do battle in Game two of the Summit Series at Maple Leaf Gardens in Toronto. The series marked the first time that Canada's best NHL players competed against the Soviets.

The Russians had played bandy – field hockey on ice – since the 1890s. In 1939, they made hockey part of the program at Moscow's Physical Culture Institute. The Soviets used the methods described by Canadian coach Lloyd Percival in his book, *The Hockey Handbook*, published in 1951 – a book that was mostly ignored in Canada. Soviet hockey boss Anatoli Tarasov was helped by the USSR's military system. Promising players went directly into the army, where they could play for the Red Army hockey team.

The Soviet system soon paid off. In 1954, the Soviets made their first appearance at the World Ice Hockey Championships. And they stunned Canada 7-2 to win the gold medal. Canada won the next year when the Penticton Vees took gold, then again in 1958 with the Whitby Dunlops, in 1959 with the Belleville McFarlands, and in 1961 with the Trail Smoke Eaters. But ever since then, the Soviets had pretty much owned the world championship title.

If Canada was going to win back world hockey bragging rights, it would have to do it without its two superstars. Fast, powerful scoring whiz Bobby Hull was banned from the tournament by the NHL because he had jumped to the

The Flower: He was known as "le Demon Blond." When Montreal Canadiens' right-winger Guy Lafleur tore down the ice with the puck, his blond hair flying, fans rose instinctively to their feet. He became the first player in NHL history to score at least 50 goals and 100 points in six consecutive seasons. His philosophy was simple: "Play every game as if it were your last."

The Thinker: Montreal Canadiens' goalie Ken Dryden became famous for standing with his arms resting on his stick when play was in the other end. He was also famous for his excellence in net. After playing just six regular season games for Montreal in 1971, he emerged as the star of the playoffs, backstopping the Canadiens to the first of six Stanley Cups in an eight-year run.

upstart World Hockey Association. And Boston Bruins genius defenseman Bobby Orr couldn't play because of a knee injury.

Even so, few Canadians doubted that their team would triumph. Newspaper reporters predicted that the Russians would be lucky to win even one of the eight games. The Soviets were Communist robots, they said, while the Canadians played hockey with love. The Soviet players knew what the Canadians thought of them. They also knew that they had nothing to lose.

At 8:00 p.m. on September 2, 1972, Prime Minister Trudeau dropped the puck in the Montreal Forum and the "Summit Series" began. Thirty seconds into the game, Phil Esposito scored Team Canada's first goal. When Paul Henderson scored again six minutes later, it looked as if Team Canada would live up to its fans' extravagant expectations. But the Soviets soon settled down and showed off their extraordinary passing, skating, and scoring skills. By the time the game ended, Canada was in shock: the Soviets had won 7-3.

In Game two, Canada fought back hard – some would say brutally – to win at Maple Leaf Gardens. The teams tied in Winnipeg. And then, when the Soviets defeated Canada 5-2 in Vancouver, the fans booed their team off the ice. Phil Esposito

The Eagle: Alan Eagleson (right) was a sports-loving lawyer who revolutionized pro hockey by helping to organize NHL players into a Players Association. The union gave the players more power when dealing with owners. It also gave Eagleson a lot of clients: he acted as agent for many players, including stars like Bobby Orr. Eagleson helped to organize international hockey tournaments such as the Summit Series and the Canada Cup, but it all went wrong when investigations revealed that he had been dishonest in his handling of money belonging to the players. The investigations resulted in criminal charges to which Eagleson pleaded guilty. He received an eighteen-month prison sentence and a $1 million fine.

made an emotional post-game speech on TV, telling Canadian fans that their team was doing its best, but the country felt betrayed. Losing was not in the plan at all.

To win the series, Team Canada had to take three of the four remaining games on enemy ice – a seemingly impossible task. They got off to a great start, at one point leading the fifth game by 4-1. But the Soviets fought back, and just like that, Canada was on the wrong end of a 5-4 score.

In Game six, the West German referees called a baffling series of penalties against Canada, and the game was rough – and about to get worse.

The Canadians had been burned by Valery Kharlamov's elegant, fearless play. His three goals and three assists were enough to motivate Canada's Bobby Clarke to swing his stick at Kharlamov's leg so hard that he broke the Soviet's ankle. To this day, the Russians remember it as a great crime. The slash put Kharlamov pretty much out of the series (though he would play in Game eight on a frozen ankle, and managed an assist).

Above: Three thousand Canadians – including hockey legend Cyclone Taylor – traveled to Moscow to support their team. During the four games in the Soviet Union, the fans became a potent part of the team.

Team Canada had another weapon: Paul Henderson. He was a streaky scorer – he got his goals in bunches. He had scored four goals in the series, two of them in Game five. Now, in Game six, his second period goal turned out to be the game winner. In the stands, the three thousand Canadian fans started to shout, "Da Da Canada, Nyet, Nyet Soviet," which meant "Yes, Yes, Canada, No, No Soviets," in Russian.

Trailblazers: Before the 1972 Summit Series, and before the debut of the Canadian national men's hockey team in 1963, Canada sent its best amateur men's ice hockey teams to the World Championships. In 1961, a team from the mining town of Trail, British Columbia, went to Switzerland to represent Canada. The Trail Smoke Eaters were named for an incident in 1929, when the town's team took a bad penalty, and fans threw things on the ice. One fan threw his pipe, which was still smoking, and a Trail player skated out with the pipe between his teeth. He was pictured in a cartoon in the *Vancouver Province* newspaper the next day, and the story that went with it called the team "a bunch of smoke eaters." Two years later, the Smoke Eaters won their first World Championship by winning eight straight games and giving up only one goal.

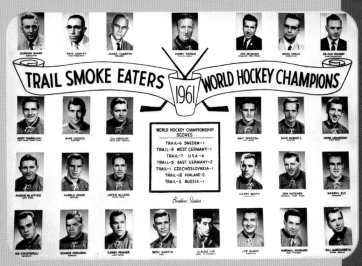

In 1961, the Smoke Eaters were in a tight spot. They were tied with the Czechs for first place. In order to win the tournament, they had to win their final game against the Soviets by at least four goals, as goal differential was the tie-breaker. In the third period of that last game, they were leading the Soviets 4-1, and needed one more goal to win the title. Time was running out when Trail's Norm Lenardon intercepted a Soviet clearing pass, and off balance, fired it home to give the Smoke Eaters a 5-1 lead, and soon, their second World Championship and the pride of a nation. Their 1961 victory marked the last time that Canada sent an amateur team to represent the country in the world championships of hockey.

The Rise and Fall of the WHA: The league started by the Patrick Brothers – the Pacific Coast Hockey Association – folded in 1924. Ever since then, the NHL reigned as the top pro hockey league in the world. But on November 1, 1971, two California businessmen, Dennis Murphy and Gary Davidson, announced the arrival of competition: the World Hockey Association. The new league began play in October 1972 with ten franchises, including Canadian cities the NHL had long ignored, such as Winnipeg, Edmonton, and Calgary. (Former NHL cities from the old days, Ottawa and Quebec City, would join the WHA later.) The owners of the new league needed a Big Name Player to give it instant credibility. They wooed thirty-three-year-old superstar Bobby Hull (right) away from the Chicago Black Hawks with a $2.75 million, ten-year contract to play for the Winnipeg Jets. The Golden Jet accepted a cheque for $1 million – an unheard of sum at the time – as his advance, and joined the WHA on June 27, 1972. The NHL responded to this new business threat by refusing to allow Bobby Hull to play for Team Canada in the 1972 Summit Series. In spite of a national campaign mounted on his behalf by disappointed fans, Hull had to watch the series from the stands. Soon other NHL legends, including Gordie Howe (above right) and Frank Mahovlich (below right), jumped to the WHA. Still, the new league was no match for the powerful NHL. The WHA folded in 1979.

The Broad Street Bullies: The Philadelphia Flyers changed the face (or broke the nose) of pro hockey in the 1970s with rough tactics that earned them the nickname "The Broad Street Bullies" (Broad Street was the address of their home arena, The Spectrum). Tired of being pushed around, the Flyers, under coach Fred Shero, put together a team of tough guys like Dave "The Hammer" Schultz, never-say-die players like Bobby Clarke, and talented goalie Bernie Parent, to create a powerful team chemistry. Critics claimed the Flyers were no better than thugs, but their rowdy approach, mixed with pure hockey talent, saw them win two straight Stanley Cups in 1974 and '75. Many other teams tried to play the same way. In this photo, Bobby Clarke tangles with Toronto's all-star defenseman Borje Salming, one of the first Swedish players in the NHL, and the first Swedish player to be inducted into the Hockey Hall of Fame.

In Game seven, there were just two minutes left in a 3-3 tie when Henderson put the puck into the net just above goalie Vladislav Tretiak's right elbow. Canadian fans went wild. With the series tied at three wins apiece and one tie, Canada now could win it all. But so could the Soviets.

And it looked as if they were going to. After two periods in Game eight, the Canadians were losing 5-3. During the intermission, the Canadian dressing room was quiet. The players knew what they had to do. At 2:27 of the third period, Phil Esposito whacked in his own rebound. Ten minutes later, Espo shook off two Soviet players to let loose a blast at Tretiak. The rebound popped out to Yvan Cournoyer, who popped it back in, and with just seven minutes left, the game was tied.

Pyramid Power versus Kate Smith: Many hockey players have long believed that putting on their equipment a certain way, or performing ritual actions during the warm-up has a direct bearing on their game. Wayne Gretzky didn't allow any sticks to cross over each other, or to touch other players' sticks. Goalie Patrick Roy would juggle pucks between periods, and then hide them to ward off bad luck. In the 1970s, the Philadelphia Flyers believed that singer Kate Smith (right) and her version of "God Bless America" gave them an edge. Former Toronto Maple Leaf player Red Kelly, as coach of the 1975-76 Leafs, put crystal pyramids in the dressing room, and under the players' bench, hoping that the energy given off by the pyramids would propel the Leafs to Stanley Cup glory. After defeating Pittsburgh, Toronto took on their fierce rivals, the Philadelphia Flyers, who eventually won a tough seven-game series – with the help of Kate Smith.

Above: A ticket to Game eight of the Summit Series in Moscow on September 28, 1972, was a valuable item. The game represented the showdown between Canada and the USSR: the winner of this game would win the series.

The Soviets, tired and rattled, probably would have settled for a tie. But Canada was playing to win. With less than a minute left to play, Henderson wanted to get on the ice. But he couldn't.

Esposito's line wouldn't come off. Henderson had to shout three times, loudly and desperately, before Peter Mahovlich skated to the bench. Esposito and Cournoyer stayed out, and Henderson dashed into the play.

Cournoyer fired a long diagonal pass just behind Henderson. Esposito beat three Soviet players to retrieve it, then fired it at Tretiak from twelve feet out. Henderson picked up the rebound and then shot the puck. Tretiak made a pad save going down. The puck came back to Henderson and he shot again. He scored.

Thirty-four seconds later it was all over. Canada had won.

Canadians would learn from the series to put more emphasis on conditioning and skill. Soon, players from Sweden and Finland would be suiting up for NHL teams. And then, in 1989, Soviet players came to the NHL, too. Some barriers between countries were broken and the game got better as a result.

As for Paul Henderson, he went back to the NHL, and then played for a while in the WHA. He never again had a run of such brilliance. But then, he didn't need to. He had been a hero when it mattered most.

The Great One

Every winter in Brantford, Ontario, Walter Gretzky flooded the backyard to make a rink for his son. He knew that his son was talented, that he might even be a hockey genius. But Walter Gretzky was leaving nothing to chance.

Walter invented drills for his son. Wayne jumped over hockey sticks while his father fed him passes. He learned to make accurate shots by aiming for the corners of the net – Walter blocked the rest off with the family picnic table laid on its side.

"When the Russians came over here in 1972 and '73," Wayne Gretzky recalled, "people said 'Wow! This is something incredible.' Not to me it wasn't. I'd been doing those drills since I was three years old. My dad was very smart."

When he was thirteen years old, after just seven years of playing organized hockey, Gretzky had scored 988 goals, and was on his way to scoring more than 1,000. And yet, he didn't look like a guy who would rewrite hockey history. He was skinny and shy. After he appeared on CBC radio's morning program, the host described the then five-foot-two Gretzky as a "solemn squirrel."

A few years later, Gretzky was playing junior hockey for the Sault Ste. Marie Greyhounds. After just seventeen games, he was leading the league with 20 goals and 35 assists – an amazing average of nearly four points a game. He went on national TV in November 1977 and he told the country his secret.

Opposite: A jubilant Wayne Gretzky poses with his fourth Stanley Cup in 1988 – and the Conn Smythe Trophy as the Stanley Cup playoff's most valuable player. With Gretzky is the nucleus of the Oilers' dynasty: coaches Glen Sather (kneeling, left) and John Muckler (kneeling, right), owner Peter Pocklington (behind the Cup), goalie Grant Fuhr (partly obscured, middle row, right), and Mark Messier (top right).

"When I'm out there I try to think as far ahead as I can," Gretzky said. "Even before the play develops, I try to think of where the puck's going to go and where to be. When I go in on goal I think about everything else but scoring."

Gretzky started his pro career with the Indianapolis Racers of the World Hockey Association. Then he moved to the Edmonton Oilers. The Oilers were playing in the WHA, but were about to make the leap to the NHL. They took Gretzky with them, giving him a twenty-one-year contract for $5 million. He signed it on his eighteenth birthday in January 1979. At the time, it was the richest contract in the history of sport.

In his first NHL season in 1979-80, Gretzky tied the Los Angeles Kings' scoring ace Marcel Dionne with 137 points for the NHL lead. (Dionne won the scoring title because he had more goals.) Gretzky was awarded the first of his eight consecutive (and nine in total) Hart Trophies as the most valuable player in the NHL. He also won the first of his five Lady Byng Trophies for most sportsmanlike play.

Number 99 played the game a whole new way. His famous ability to see the whole of the ice was something people had to learn how to watch. It sometimes seemed that Gretzky was skating into empty space. And then the puck would appear where Gretzky knew it would be. And then it was in the opposing net.

He liked to set up behind the opponents' goal in a space that sportswriters began to call his "office." If an opponent moved in to check him from one side, he moved out the other. If two opponents pinched in from both sides, that meant two of his teammates were open. Gretzky was a threat even when he seemed to be doing nothing.

And Gretzky had some great teammates. Mark Messier, Glenn Anderson, Jari Kurri, Paul Coffey, Esa Tikkanen, and goalie Grant Fuhr all grew better together to form a championship team. With them were tough guys Dave Semenko and Marty McSorley. Their job was to make sure their opponents left Gretzky alone so he could do what he did best. Play hockey.

And Gretzky kept breaking records. In March 1981, he notched three assists in a 5-2 Edmonton win over Pittsburgh to smash Phil Esposito's record of 152 points. Two days later

Brothers in Arms: In the early 1980s, Czechoslovakia (now two countries, the Czech Republic and Slovakia) was a totalitarian communist state. Three hockey-playing brothers, Marian, Peter, and Anton Stastny (pictured left to right above), escaped to Canada to play for the Quebec Nordiques. The defection caused much grief in Czechoslovakia, especially when Peter played for Canada in the 1984 Canada Cup. But Stastny had become a Canadian citizen and wanted to play for his new country. Together, the brothers anchored the Nordiques. They never won the Stanley Cup, but Peter Stastny's hockey excellence was recognized by his induction to the Hockey Hall of Fame in 1998.

King in Exile: Marcel Dionne was always unconventional. Because of hometown pressures and because he wanted to learn English, he rejected a junior career in his home province of Quebec, and played instead for St. Catharines, Ontario. When he made it to the NHL, centerman Dionne made his mark as a scoring wizard for the Los Angeles Kings. This was at a time – before Gretzky's arrival – when hockey was almost invisible in Southern California. Even so, Dionne beat Wayne Gretzky for the league scoring title in 1980. When he retired in 1989, he was third in the history of NHL scoring, behind Gretzky and Gordie Howe.

Above right: Wayne Gretzky, parked near his "office" behind the Philadelphia net, and Jari Kurri (number 17) formed one of the most potent scoring duos the NHL has ever known. As Gretzky's right-winger, Kurri was a complete player: he could score goals as easily as he could defend against them. In 1984-85, Kurri scored 71 goals and 135 points, setting a single season record for a right-winger. He finished second in the scoring race to Gretzky, and the Oilers won their second straight Stanley Cup.

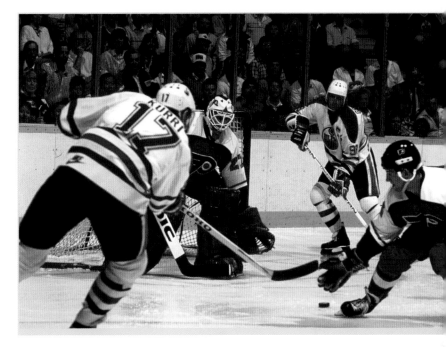

he broke Bobby Orr's record of 102 assists, on his way to a whopping 164 point season: 55 goals, and 109 assists.

But he was just getting started. The following season, on December 30, 1981, Gretzky scored five goals against Philadelphia to reach the 50-goal mark in 39 games, the fastest in NHL history. Two months later, in a game against Buffalo, Gretzky scored three goals to break Phil Esposito's record of 76 en route to an unheard of 92 goals and 120 assists. Wayne Gretzky had become the first NHL player to cross the impossible 200-point threshold in a single campaign.

The Edmonton Oilers knew that he was worth more than they were paying him, so they tore up his old contract, and negotiated a new one. This one would see him earn $20 million over fifteen years, as well as a piece of a shopping mall. The Oilers promised that Gretzky would be an Oiler for the rest of his hockey career.

In May 1984, Gretzky led the Oilers to their first of his four Stanley Cups. As if he hadn't achieved enough, Canadians now looked to him to lead Team Canada to victory in the 1984 Canada Cup tournament.

Three years earlier, Team Canada had been humiliated by a powerful Soviet team. Gretzky had been a member of that

The Canada Cup: Montreal Canadiens' speedy scoring wizard Steve Shutt goes airborne in the inaugural Canada Cup while Canadian teammate – and Montreal linemate – Peter Mahovlich looks on. The Canada Cup tournament brought together teams from the best hockey-playing nations once every four years. The first series was played in 1976 when Canada beat the Czechs by winning the first two games of the three-game final series to claim the new trophy. The next Canada Cup was played in 1981 (it was delayed a year because of the Soviet invasion of Afghanistan) and the Soviets thumped Canada in the final. Tournament organizer Alan Eagleson wouldn't let the Soviets take the trophy home. To make up for Eagleson's petulant display of poor sportsmanship, a Winnipeg man, George Smith, asked Canadians to donate money to make a new trophy. He soon found himself with $32,000 worth of donations, and the astonished Soviets were touched when they received their replica trophy. The Canada Cup continued as a tournament until 1991 – Canada won every championship after 1981. It was replaced in 1996 by the World Cup of Hockey.

"Big Bird": Larry Robinson was an intimidating six-foot-four, 225-pound defenseman who patroled the blue line for the Montreal Canadiens for seventeen seasons. He then added three more years with the Los Angeles Kings. He was awarded the Norris Trophy twice as the league's best defenseman, but he was also a skilled puck handler who racked up 958 career points during the regular season, and another 144 during the playoffs. When he retired in 1992, Robinson became a coach, and won two more Stanley Cups behind the bench for New Jersey in addition to the six he had won on the ice with Montreal.

Right: A young Wayne Gretzky watches the action from the bench. It was said of him that he could see plays developing in his head before they actually happened on the ice.

The Coach: He is the coach with the most wins in NHL history – 1,244. To that he can add nine Stanley Cups, and a generation of players and coaches who learned from him, and often were beaten by him. Scotty Bowman was prevented from playing pro hockey because of a head injury when he was a junior, but it was his brain that made him a legend. His coaching strategies were refined through twenty-seven years in the NHL, where he never had a losing record. He was well-traveled, too, as the bench boss of St. Louis, Montreal, Buffalo, Pittsburgh, and Detroit. It was in Detroit in 1997 that he guided the Red Wings to their first Stanley Cup championship in forty-two years.

Canadian team, but now he had help from his Stanley Cup-winning teammates. The team that had won Lord Stanley's trophy set out to restore Canada's international hockey reputation

Things looked bad in the early going. At the end of the first round, the Soviets boasted a perfect 5-0 record, while Canada had broken even at 2-2-1. And just as worrying, their shaky fourth-place finish in round-robin play had earned them a place in the semifinals – against the Soviets.

The game went into overtime. Canada's Paul Coffey broke up a Soviet two-on-one, and then Coffey – the smoothest skater in the league – took off down the ice. He fired a puck at the Soviet goalie that was deflected into the net by teammate Mike Bossy. Team Canada went on to defeat a tough Swedish team in the two-game final.

Gretzky was named to the tournament's all-star team, and finished first in scoring, with 5 goals and 7 assists over eight games. Canadians now had reason to hope for a long and happy international hockey reign. Gretzky was twenty-three years old.

Life after Gretzky: After Wayne Gretzky was traded to Los Angeles in 1988, Edmonton fans thought they had seen the last of the Stanley Cup. But two seasons later the Oilers, led by captain Mark Messier (with Cup), and teammates Esa Tikkanen and Joe Murphy, defeated the Boston Bruins to bring Edmonton its fifth Stanley Cup in seven years.

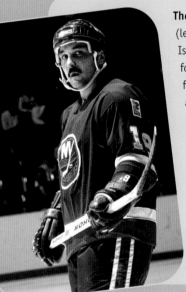

The Islanders: Led by the great two-way center Bryan Trottier (left) and sniper Mike Bossy (right) on right wing, the New York Islanders were the hockey dynasty of the early 1980s. They won four straight Stanley Cups from 1980 to 1983, becoming the first team from the United States to win three Cups or more in a row. After scoring an all-time rookie high of 53 goals in his first NHL season, Mike Bossy followed up with two more 50-goal seasons. In the 1980-81 season, Bossy set his sights on the one record that had stood untouched since 1945: Rocket Richard's 50 goals in 50 games. Tension was high when the third period began in Game fifty, and Bossy was still stuck at 49 goals. But then, with less than two minutes left in the game, Bossy took a pass from Trottier and scored on the Quebec Nordiques to match the Rocket's seemingly unbreakable record.

Miracle on Ice: 1980 was a tough year for Americans. They were still emotionally bruised by the loss of Vietnam to communists. Some of their citizens were held as hostages in Iran by a hostile new government. And the Soviets had just invaded Afghanistan. The USA needed a boost to its self-esteem.

The Winter Olympic Games that year were held in Lake Placid, New York, but not many observers gave the US men's hockey team much of a chance, even with home ice advantage. Their team was a bunch of no-names. And yet, inspired by the tough-love motivation of coach Herb Brooks, the USA Squad made Miracle Number One by defeating the powerhouse Soviets in a 4-3 semifinal game, one that was seen as nothing less then American democracy versus Soviet communism. And then, inspired by patriotic fervor, the United States team made Miracle Number Two by defeating Finland 4-2 to win hockey gold. A generation of American kids took up hockey because of the Miracle on Ice.

Slick Speedster: Scotty Bowman once described defenseman Paul Coffey as "a fourth forward." Coffey's stride was so smooth that opponents often didn't realize how fast he was going until he had blown past them. With his hard shot, Coffey could also put the puck in the net. He was effective in his own end too: he won the Norris Trophy three times as the NHL's best defenseman. He was a key member of the Edmonton Oilers' Stanley Cup dynasty of the 1980s.

And then came the news that shocked the country. In the summer of 1988, just after he married American actress Janet Jones in a glamorous wedding, a tearful Gretzky announced that he had agreed to be traded to the Los Angeles Kings. The Edmonton Oilers were in financial trouble and their owner, Peter Pocklington, saw Gretzky as a valuable commodity to be sold for a lot of money. So on August 9, Gretzky and two of his teammates went to Los Angeles in exchange for two Kings, three first-round draft picks, and $20 million in cash. The kid who set a new standard in hockey salaries was sold because he was worth so much.

Gretzky helped to make NHL hockey more popular in the United States. Fans getting tans on California beaches wore Kings jerseys with number 99 and "Gretzky" on the back. At home, Canadians dared to hope that he would one day return and bring hockey glory with him. Gretzky would do just that but, true to form, he would do it his own way.

Mario and Manon

Just as Walter Gretzky built Wayne an ice rink, so did Mario Lemieux's mother. But hers was a little different. It was not in the Lemieux family's backyard – it was *inside* the house.

She would shovel snow from her yard and dump it in the front hallway. She'd pat it down into a hard surface, then leave the doors open so it would freeze. And then Mario would skate on this little rink in the hallway. Soon, though, there would be no rink big enough to contain his talent.

When Manon Rheaume – just a few years younger than Mario – was a little girl living near Quebec City, she wanted to play hockey at the highest level, too. That meant playing with boys. When her father needed a goalie for the boys' team he was coaching, Manon said she knew the perfect player. Herself.

To avoid attracting attention, they decided they wouldn't tell anyone she was a girl. "And the first time, just to make sure that people would not judge me because I was a girl, they dressed me at home," she said. "Put my helmet on and I went on the ice and not a lot of people noticed."

But a lot of people would notice Mario and Manon, for each in their own way changed hockey.

Lemieux first came to the hockey world's attention when he refused to play for Canada in the 1984 World Junior Championship. He said the series would hurt his chances of winning the league-scoring championship. A lot of fans were angered because he put his own interests ahead of his country's.

Opposite: As the first woman to play in the NHL, goalie Manon Rheaume was a hockey pioneer. Her accomplishment focused attention on the women's game.

He attracted attention again when he refused to pull on a sweater. The Pittsburgh Penguins made him the first pick in the 1984 amateur draft and Lemieux refused to have his picture taken in a Penguins jersey. It was his way of telling the Penguins that they weren't offering him enough money. He wanted a million dollars.

Mario took a lot of flak for this apparently selfish gesture. But he knew he was good. In his last season in junior hockey with the Laval Voisins, he had scored a staggering 133 goals and collected 282 points. Still, a million dollars for a rookie was pushing it. Eventually, a deal was worked out that made both sides happy. Mario could earn a million when "bonus money" kicked in. He just had to prove that he was as good as he thought he was.

So all he did was score in his first shift in his first NHL game. Then he won the Calder Trophy as Rookie of the Year. Even though the Penguins finished out of the playoffs, Lemieux gave their fans hope.

Lemieux also won over some fans when he agreed to play for Team Canada in the 1987 Canada Cup. This would be the first time he found himself wearing the maple leaf insignia on the ice with Gretzky, and Lemieux had something to prove.

The Captain: Steve Yzerman won NHL respect early: He became the youngest captain in Detroit Red Wings history in the 1986-87 season. The 21-year-old center responded to the responsibility by leading the team in scoring for seven straight years. In five of those years, he scored more than 50 goals. Yzerman led the Wings to three Stanley Cups, and was a key player on Canada's gold medal winning team at the Salt Lake City Olympics.

Opposite: Mario the Magnificent uses his size to muscle a Chicago Black Hawk off the puck. Despite his superb physical strength, Lemieux usually preferred to use dekes and speed to get past opponents.

Pretty in Pink: After decades of neglect, Canadian women finally got a chance to compete in the world's first international women's hockey tournament in Ottawa in March 1990. Canada's TSN (The Sports Network) televised four games nationally. About eighty-five journalists from six countries came to cover the most important tournament in women's hockey. The event featured teams from Sweden, Finland, Norway, West Germany, Switzerland, Japan, and the USA. But when the Canadian women walked into the dressing room to pull on their country's jerseys, they were horrified to see that they were pink. Just as insulting to the serious female players was the fact that beauty makeovers were awarded as door prizes to fans. By the time the tournament was over, the "Pink Ladies" had shown that the maple leaf on their sweaters was what mattered. They outscored their European opponents 32-1, and they had defeated Japan 18-0. After spotting two goals to the United States in the championship game, the Canadians stormed back with five unanswered goals to win the gold.

Team Canada lost the first match to the Soviets in the three-game final. In the second game, Lemieux turned on the jets. He scored a hat trick, all assisted by Gretzky. His third goal, a dramatic masterpiece in the tenth minute of the second overtime period, tied the series.

The championship match was played in Hamilton. With the game tied at 5, and less than two minutes left in regulation time, Lemieux had yet to find the back of the net, and both he and Gretzky were on the ice for a face-off in the Canadian zone. The Soviets won the face-off. Lemieux, whose six-foot-four, 230-pound frame made him seem much slower than he was,

Saint Patrick: They called him "Saint Patrick" because he performed goaltending miracles. Roy grew up as a fan of the Quebec Nordiques. He hated Montreal, but they drafted him fifty-first overall in 1984. It was as a Canadien that he first showed the hockey world his amazing ability. He won two Cups with the Habs. Roy could stretch like a cat to snatch a seemingly sure goal out of midair, or he could stand square to the shooter and stare him down. It helped that his pads got bigger each season. In November 1995, the Montreal coach, with whom he had been arguing, left Roy in net as nine goals were scored on him in a game that ended in a 12-1 win for Detroit. Roy was stung by the humiliation and demanded to be traded. He got his wish and was sent to Colorado. He helped backstop the Avalanche to a Stanley Cup that very season. He retired in 2003 with a staggering 551 wins, the most for a goalie in NHL history.

used his long reach to poke the puck away from the Soviet player, and shovel it into the clear for Gretzky. The two super-stars took off. Defenseman Larry Murphy joined them in a three-on-two rush.

The fans were on their feet, screaming, as Gretzky crossed the blue line with the puck, hugging the boards, and taking a Soviet player with him. Murphy moved to the net and took another defender with him, which meant Lemieux was in the open. The all-seeing Gretzky fed him a perfect tape-to-tape pass. Lemieux fired it into the top corner, glove side, of the Soviet net. Canada had won in heroic, last-minute fashion, and Lemieux had put to rest an old ghost. "What can be a greater thrill than scoring the two winning goals against the Russians?" he said. "I think I have answered some questions about me in this tournament."

A question remained in many fans' minds about how good he really was in comparison to Gretzky. In the following season, he answered by beating Gretzky to win the first of his five Art Ross Trophies as the NHL's leading point-getter. He also won the first of his three Hart Trophies as the league's most valuable player. And in 1991, despite an agonizing back injury, Lemieux led the Penguins to their first of two consecutive Stanley Cup championships.

Just when he was at the top of his game, Lemieux faced the hardest challenge of all. In December 1992, he was diagnosed with Hodgkin's disease – a form of cancer.

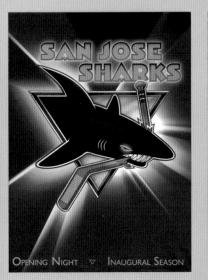

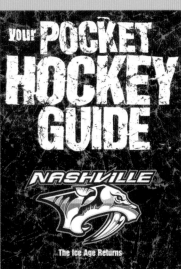

Expansion: In the autumn of 1993, The Disney Corporation upset hockey purists by icing an NHL expansion team named after one of their movies. The movie was a 1992 hit about a sleazy lawyer who is arrested for drunk driving. He is sentenced to community service as coach of a misfit hockey team called the Mighty Ducks. The team jersey of the real-life Anaheim Mighty Ducks featured an angry duck face and the team played their home games at The Pond. Just the same, the arrival of the Anaheim team was much more than a cute publicity stunt. The NHL was serious about taking the game of hockey to the United States. The Ducks joined other expansion teams San Jose and Miami, as well as Ottawa, which had a long hockey tradition. Within another ten years, there were teams in a number of locations where hockey was a novelty, such as Nashville and the Carolinas, as well as in hockey-savvy Minnesota and Columbus.

Lemieux underwent radiation treatment for four weeks. Such therapy often has harsh side effects, including terrible fatigue, but Lemieux's conditioning served him well. After his final treatment on March 2, 1993, with the radiation burn still fresh on his neck, Lemieux flew to Philadelphia to rejoin the Penguins. That night, after a ninety-second ovation from the tough Philadelphia fans, he celebrated his survival by scoring a goal and adding an assist.

Mario Lemieux's example inspired so many American kids to take up hockey that they became known as "The Mario Generation." Manon Rheaume was not a superstar in the same league as Mario – how could she be, with no pro-hockey league for women? – but she, too, turned a generation of young women onto hockey.

Rheaume was the first woman to play in a junior hockey game when she suited up for the Trois-Rivières Draveurs of the Quebec Major Junior League. Tapes of her performance made it to Phil Esposito, general manager of the Tampa Bay Lightning,

Above: Manon Rheaume celebrates victory over Team USA in March 1990.

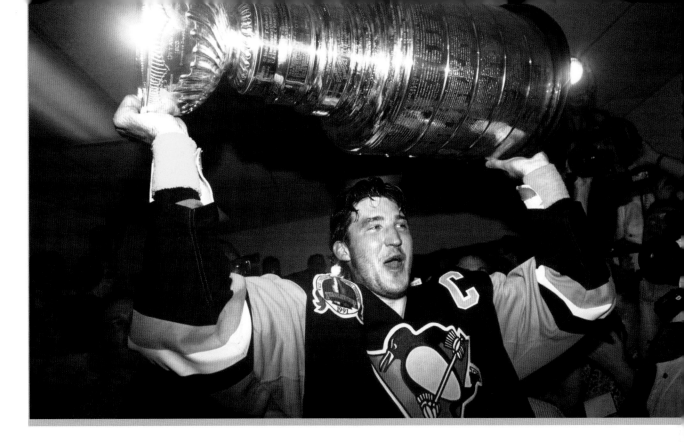

Above: Lemieux celebrates his and Pittsburgh's first-ever Stanley Cup win in 1991. Despite crippling back injuries, Lemieux returned to the lineup late in the season, picking up 44 points in 23 games, and the Conn Smythe Trophy as the most valuable player in the Stanley Cup playoffs.

and he was impressed. Then his scouts told him that Rheaume was female. "I guess that made Phil look at the tape differently," said Rheaume. "For the first time being a girl was a good thing."

Esposito, trying to sell a cold sport in Florida's hot climate, saw not only a good goalie, but a brilliant marketing opportunity. And so Manon Rheaume found herself playing in an NHL exhibition game against St. Louis. She became the first woman to play in the world's premier hockey league.

Rheaume, along with fifteen-year-old Hayley Wickenheiser, was part of the Canadian women's team that won gold in the world championships in 1994. Rheaume made history again in 1998, as a member of the first Canadian team to play in the first women's Olympic hockey tournament in Nagano, Japan. Mario Lemieux was there, too, for now Canada was sending its best players, and had a shot at winning double gold. Many Canadian fans were so sure of victory that, as in some earlier years, they started celebrating too soon. And, as had happened before, they were in for a rude surprise.

CHAPTER TEN

Gold in the Ice

F or many Canadians, the 1998 Winter Olympic Games at Nagano, Japan, were a nightmare. To be sure, the Canadian women's hockey team won silver, but they felt in their hearts that they were good enough to win gold.

And for the men's national team, gold had turned to lead. More than a million Canadians watched in horror as Team Canada lost in an overtime shootout to the Czech Republic in the semifinal. The stunned Canadians then went on to lose the bronze medal match to Finland. "Any time you put on the uniform, anything less than the gold medal is unacceptable," said Gretzky. "This is the only country in the world where that's true."

International hockey had come a long way from the days when Frank Frederickson and his Winnipeg Falcons could give away goals to grateful foreigners. Now, teams from Sweden, the Czech Republic, Finland, and Russia all were able to call on players from NHL teams to fill out their national squads. And then there was Team USA, a hockey powerhouse that had achieved its own Olympic success in 1980 – the "Miracle on Ice." Today, some of the NHL's best players hold American passports.

So, for the 2002 Olympics in Salt Lake City, Canadian organizers recruited some serious firepower. Wayne Gretzky, who had retired from the NHL in 1999, would be back as general manager. Mario Lemieux would be back, too: he had "unretired."

Opposite: Team Canada's executive director Wayne Gretzky proudly holds up the one-dollar Canadian coin that became known as the "Lucky Loonie."

Left: The Canadian women's Olympic hockey team celebrates its first-ever Olympic gold medal at Salt Lake City, 2002.

Lemieux had hung up his skates in 1997. But then he got bad news. The financially troubled Pittsburgh Penguins couldn't pay him the money they owed him, and it was a lot: $33 million.

So Lemieux did something that no other professional sports player had yet done: he bought his old team as part of an ownership group. In order to put fans back in the seats, he pulled on his old number 66 jersey, and stepped back onto the ice.

Although Lemieux's return on December 27, 2000, came after almost four years of retirement, he soon showed that he meant business. Just thirty-three seconds into the game against Toronto, he set up a goal, and later scored, as the Penguins shut out the Leafs 5-0. "He's a suit-wearing executive by day," marveled a Penguins' executive. "At night he puts on his cape and plays."

After their disaster at Nagano, the men's hockey team needed a caped superhero. Lemieux's mission was to find gold in the ice and bring it home.

Trent Evans was also thinking about Olympic gold.

As ice-makers for the Edmonton Oilers, Evans and his crew were famous throughout the NHL. The organizers of the Salt Lake City Olympics invited Evans and a couple of his colleagues to become part of an elite international crew of ice-makers and Zamboni drivers. These people would ensure that the best hockey players in the world had the best ice to play on.

The logo embedded in the ice in the middle of the arena in Salt Lake City had no center mark. Evans had to locate the exact center so he could make sure the nets and other markings were

The Soviet Invasion: The Berlin Wall had separated the Communist East from the democratic West all through the Cold War. Russian players like Alexander Mogilny had to secretly escape from their home country in order to earn a salary in North America. Mogilny signed with Buffalo in 1989. That same year, the Berlin Wall was taken down. Now players from communist countries were free to play in the NHL. Sergei Priakin was the first Soviet player allowed to join an NHL club: he signed with the Calgary Flames in 1989. Soon Russian stars such as Sergei Makarov (above), Igor Larionov, and Slava Fetisov (right) were lighting up the NHL and changing the North American game with their precision-passing skills. They, in turn, were followed by the next generation of stars: Pavel Bure, Sergei Federov, Ilya Kovalchuk, and Alexander Ovechkin. Ironically, during the NHL lockout of 2004-05, many NHL players went to Russia to play hockey.

in the right place. Normally, he would drill a screw into the ice, but he didn't have a screw. He had a Canadian dime, so he set the dime into the ice and used that.

That evening, while talking to his fellow ice-maker, Duncan Muire, he came up with an idea for an even better marker. "We both agreed that it would be better to have the gold of a loonie," said Evans, "because we wanted the teams to win gold, and not the silver of a dime."

Evans placed the one-dollar Canadian coin – called a "loonie" because it bears the image of a Canadian bird, the loon – on top of the dime at center ice, and then he flooded the rink.

You could still see the loonie beneath center ice if you looked hard. When the people supervising his work told him to remove the loonie, Evans couldn't bring himself to do it. So he painted a yellow spot on top of it, and hoped that would do the trick – once the Canadian teams knew about it.

Evans told the Canadian women's team himself. They were facing their archrivals, the United States, and they were delighted. They were convinced the loonie would help them win gold. They needed all the help they could get.

The Canadian women had lost a troubling eight straight pre-Olympic matches to the United States. And they had problems with Finland in the semifinal before coming from behind to win 7-3.

The game against the United States proved to be as tough as expected. The referee – a woman *and* an American – called thirteen penalties against Canada, eight of them in a row, while giving Team USA only six. Still the Canadians – with the loonie beneath their skates – withstood a last-minute rally to win gold. "It was the most emotional moment in my life," said Canadian star forward Hayley Wickenheiser. "Everything I had worked for, hoped for, came together at that moment. I was the happiest person on earth."

The existence of the loonie was a secret known only to the Canadian teams and a few associates. Evans and Gretzky had

The Quebec Summit: Every year more than 2,000 Pee Wee hockey players from sixteen countries descend upon Quebec City for the World Championships. During the eleven-day tournament, more than 200,000 hockey fans watch the next wave of NHL stars show their stuff as eleven- and twelve-year-olds. The tournament was founded in 1960. Over the years it has showcased the hockey talents of such future titans as Guy Lafleur, Marcel Dionne, Wayne Gretzky, Mario Lemieux, and Eric Lindros.

Left: Team Canada's Geraldine Heaney, Therese Brisson, and Danielle Goyette check out the lucky loonie, buried beneath the Salt Lake City Olympic ice, after their historic gold-medal win. Up in the stands, Wayne Gretzky was frantically trying to move them away from Canada's secret weapon. The men's team still had to play their gold medal game – and the loonie had to stay buried. It did.

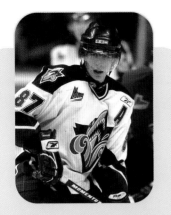

The Next One: Sidney Crosby entered the NHL with a lot of pressure on his eighteen-year-old shoulders. He was drafted in 2005 by the troubled Pittsburgh Penguins to play with owner-player Mario Lemieux. Crosby is expected to help revive the franchise much as Lemieux did twenty-one years earlier – before Crosby was born. He has been praised lavishly by the likes of Gretzky and Lemieux. Crosby, like other budding superstars before him, will have to raise the level of his game to live up to his superstar billing.

to shoo members of the women's team away from center ice immediately after the game, when some of them wanted to take a closer look.

A TV journalist reporting on the ice-making at the Olympics learned about the buried loonie. For a reporter, the story was too good to keep secret, and the story was broadcast just before the men's gold-medal game against – who else? – the United States.

But the loonie was still safe. While the Canadian men's team knew about it, the millions of Canadians who stopped to watch on the afternoon of February 24 had no idea that the puck was being dropped on such a powerful good-luck charm.

It was a classic match-up. With Canada hanging onto a 3-2 lead in the third period, the game could have gone either way. Team USA came close to tying the game when Brett Hull got a glorious chance on a power play, but Canadian goalie Martin Brodeur stopped him. Then, with four minutes left, Canada's Jarome Iginla took a snap shot that US goalie Mike Richter – sliding across the crease – had to reach back to stop. The puck hit his glove and spun end over end toward the empty net.

Joe Sakic, Iginla's centerman, tried to deflect the puck, but missed. US defenseman Tom Poti tried to sweep it out of harm's way, but missed. And when the puck dropped inside the post, it was a goal. More than 10 million Canadians watching this most-watched-ever Canadian TV event let out a roar. The game wasn't over, but it was now Canada's to lose. Joe Sakic made fools of any doubters with another goal to give Canada a 5-2 gold-medal win.

Jaromir the Magnificent: If you scramble the letters of his first name to form an anagram, Mario Jr. is the result. That's what hockey fans called Jaromir Jagr when he came to the Pittsburgh Penguins from his home in the Czech Republic in October 1990. Jagr and Lemieux played together in his first season. By the end of it, Jagr led all rookies in playoff scoring, and won his first Stanley Cup. Jagr, big and strong, soon dominated the NHL with his puck-handling skills. He won his first of four Art Ross Trophies as the league's top scorer in 1995.

Once again, Canada was on top of the hockey world – a world that had embraced the Canadian game. There would be many countries and teams and players vying for hockey supremacy in the years to come, but in the end, hockey itself would be the winner. Players young and old all over the world would ask for just one thing in winter: ice time. Give them that, and they would etch their own triumphs into the ice of the rinks of the world.

Above: In 1998, the Olympic Games welcomed professional hockey players for the first time. Canada's best NHLers went in search of hockey gold only to return home empty-handed, and in shock. Four years later they triumphed, defeating the United States to win the country's first Olympic hockey gold in fifty years.

Acknowledgments

Ice Time was made possible by the brilliant work of many. These are the stars of the game: Karen Bower at the CBC for expertly putting the team together; Jonathan Webb for his smooth editing; Natalie Tedesco, Paul Patskou, and Angela Comelli for their "nothing is impossible" researching; Kathy Lowinger for publishing it all; my wife, Nancy, for her great coaching; and my teammates at the CBC and at Tundra Books, who brought their A-game to this project, and made my job such a pleasure.

Index

Abel, Sid, 38
Allan Cup, 22, 23
Allan, Sir Hugh, 22
Anderson, Glenn, 58
Antoine, Alec, 30
Armstrong, George "Chief," 42-44, 47
Art Ross Trophy, 38, 42, 48, 68, 77
Avalanche (Colorado), 68

Bain, Dan, 11
Baker, Hobart Amory "Hobey," 24
Baptie, Norval, 13
Bathgate, Andy, 45
Bauer, Bobby, 45
Bauer, Father David, 45
Béliveau, Jean, 42, 47
Benedict, Clint, 45
Black Hawks (Chicago), 33, 37, 44, 53
Blackhawks (Chicago), 67
Blake, Hector "Toe," 35
Blue Jackets (Columbus), 69
Bossy, Mike, 61
Boucher, William "Billy," 32
Bower, Johnny, 36, 42, 43
Bowman, Scotty, 61, 63
Boyle, Joseph "Joe," 9-10
Brisson, Therese, 76
"Broad Street Bullies," 54
Brodeur, Martin, 77
Brooks, Herb, 63
Bruins (Boston), 39, 46, 62
Bure, Pavel, 75

Calder Trophy, 66
Calder, Frank, 25
Canada (national team), 22-24, 49-52, 59, 61, 66-68, 73, 76-78
Canada Cup, 58, 59, 66-68
Canadian Amateur Hockey Association (CAHA), 22
Canadian Broadcasting Corporation (CBC), 39, 57
Canadiens (Montreal), 13, 16, 19, 31, 32, 35, 36, 41-44, 45, 47, 50, 51, 60, 68
Chabot, Lorne, 29
Clancy, Francis "King," 29-30
Clarke, Bobby, 52, 54

Coffey, Paul, 58, 61, 63
Conn Smythe Trophy, 46, 57, 71
Costello, Father Les, 44
Cournoyer, Yvan "Roadrunner," 42, 54, 55
Creamery Kings (Renfrew), 15-16
Creighton, James, 7-8
Crosby, Sidney, 77
Cullen, Brian, 37
Czech Republic (national team), 73, 77
Czechoslovakia (national team), 23, 60

Davidson, Gary, 53
Dionne, Marcel, 58, 59, 76
Dominion Challenge Trophy, See Stanley Cup
Dryden, Ken, 51
Dumart, Woody, 45
Dunlops (Whitby), 50

Eagleson, Alan "Eagle," 52, 60
Esposito, Phil "Espo," 48, 49, 51, 54, 55, 58, 59, 70-71
Evans, Trent, 74-76

Falcons (Winnipeg), 15, 21-24, 73
Federov, Sergei, 75
Ferguson, Elmer, 25
Ferguson, John, 42
Fetisov, Slava, 75
Finland (national team), 67, 73
Flames (Calgary), 75
Flyers (Philadelphia), 41, 54, 55
Flying Fathers, 44
Forrest, Albert, 10-11,
Français Volants, 33
Frederickson, Frank, 20-24, 73
Fuhr, Grant, 57, 58

Gaudette, Roger, 33
Gibson, Doc, 8
Goyette, Danielle, 76
Gretzky, Walter, 57, 65
Gretzky, Wayne, 2, 55, 56-61, 62, 63, 66, 67, 68, 72-72, 76, 77
Griffiths, Si, 15
Gusev, Alexander, 48-49

Hart Trophy, 38, 42, 58, 68
Heaney, Geraldine, 76
Henderson, Paul, 49, 51, 52, 55
Hewitt, Foster, 15, 33
Hewitt, W.A., 14, 15
Hillman, Larry, 38
Hockey Night in Canada, 39
Hodge, Charlie, 43
Hoffman, Abigail, 37
Horton, Tim, 2, 42, 44
Howe, Gordie, 38, 53, 59
Hull, Brett, 70, 77
Hull, Robert "Bobby," 50, 53, 70

Iginla, Jarome, 77
Imlach, George "Punch," 44
International Hockey League (IHL), 8, 15
International Women's Hockey Tournament (1990), 67
Irvin, Dick, 35
Islanders (New York), 62

Jagr, Jaromir, 77
Johnson, Ernie "Moose," 17
Joliat, Aurele, 31, 32
Jones, Janet, 63

Kelly, "Red," 42, 44, 47, 55
Kharlamov, Valery, 52
Kings (Los Angeles), 58, 59, 60, 63
Kovalchuk, Ilya, 75
"Kraut Line," 45
Kurri, Jari, 58, 59

Lach, Elmer, 35, 37
Lady Byng Trophy, 58
Lafleur, Guy, 50, 76
Lalonde, Edouard "Newsy," 13, 16, 36
Laperriere, Jacques, 43
Larianov, Igor, 75
Laviolette, Jack, 19
Lemieux, Mario, 65-68, 70-71, 73, 76, 77
Lenardon, Norm, 53
Lesueur, Percy, 16, 19
Lightning (Tampa Bay), 70

Lindros, Eric, 76
Lindsay, Ted, 38
Livingston, Edward, 25

Mahovlich, Frank, 53
Mahovlich, Peter, 55, 60
Makarov, Sergei, 75
Malone, Joe, 37
Maple Leaf Gardens (Toronto), 15, 30, 33, 42, 50, 51
Maple Leafs (Toronto), 2, 27, 29-31, 33, 35, 36, 37, 41-44, 47, 49, 55, 74
Maroons (Montreal), 45
Maxwell, Fred "Steamer," 22
McFarlands (Belleville), 50
McGee, Frank "One-Eyed," 10-11, 15
McGill University, 5, 28
McKee, Father Brian, 44
McSorley, Marty, 58
Memorial Cup, 45
Messier, Mark, 57, 58, 62
Mighty Ducks (Anaheim), 69
Mikita, Stan, 44
Millionaires (Renfrew), 13
Millionaires (Vancouver), 19
"Miracle on Ice," 63, 73
Mogilny, Alexander, 75
Monarchs (Winnipeg), 22
Montreal Amateur Athletic Association (MAAA), 8, 9
Montreal Hockey Club, 9
Morenz, Howie, 31, 32, 45
Morrison, Jim, 37
Muckler, John, 57
Muire, Duncan, 75
Murphy, Dennis, 53
Murphy, Joe, 62
Murphy, Larry, 68

Nagano. See Winter Olympic Games (1998)
National Hockey Association (NHA), 16, 19, 25
National Hockey League (NHL), 25, 28, 32, 35, 38, 41, 49, 58, 63, 69, 75
Naylor, Tommy, 42
Nordiques (Quebec), 58, 62, 68

Norris Trophy, 46, 60, 63
Nuggets (Dawson City), 9-11,

O'Ree, Willie, 39
Oilers (Edmonton), 58, 59, 62, 63, 74
Olympic Games (1920), 22-24.
    See also Winter Olympic Games
Ontario Hockey Association (OHA), 14, 15
"Original Six," 41
Orr, Robert "Bobby," 46, 51, 52, 59
Ottawa Hockey Club, 10
Ovechkin, Alexander, 75

Pacific Coast Hockey Association (PCHA), 16, 17, 19, 21, 32, 53
Panthers (Florida), 69
Parent, Bernie, 54
Patrick, Frank, 13, 16, 17, 19
Patrick, Lester, 13, 16, 17, 19, 30
Pearson, Lester B., 4
Penguins (Pittsburgh), 66, 68, 70, 74, 77
Percival, Lloyd, 50
Phillips, Tom, 15
Pitre, Didier "Cannonball," 19
Plante, Jacques, 45
Pocklington, Peter, 57, 63
Poti, Tom, 77
Predators (Nashville), 69
Preston Rivulettes, 25
Priakin, Sergei, 75
"Production Line," 38
Pronovost, Marcel, 42
Pulford, Bob, 43, 44, 47
"Punch Line," 35

Racers (Indianapolis), 58
Rangers (New York), 2, 28, 29, 30, 45
Ranscombe, Hilda, 25
Ranscombe, Nellie, 25
Red Wings (Detroit), 37, 38, 61, 66
Regan, Larry, 42
Renaud, Gerald, 39
Rheaume, Manon, 64-65, 70-71
Richard, Henri "Pocket Rocket," 42
Richard, Maurice "Rocket," 34-37, 39, 42, 62
Richter, Mike, 77
Rideau Rebels (Ottawa), 7-8
Robinson, Larry "Big Bird," 60
Ross Cup, 24
Ross, Arthur "Art," 19. See also Art Ross Trophy
Roy, Patrick, 55, 68
Russia (national team), 73. *See also* Soviet Union

Sabres (Buffalo), 2
Sakic, Joe, 77
Salming, Borje, 54
Sather, Glen, 57
Sawchuk, Terry, 42, 43
Schmidt, Milt, 45
Schultz, Dave "The Hammer," 54
Selke, Frank, 30
Semenko, Dave, 58
Senators (Ottawa), 9, 11, 15-16, 30, 69
Sharks (San Jose), 69
Shero, Fred, 54
Shutt, Steve, 60
"Silver Seven" (Ottawa), 10-11
Smith, George, 60

Smith, Kate, 55
Smoke Eaters (Trail), 50, 53
Smythe, Constantine Falkland Cary "Conn," 26-30, 33, 42.
Smythe, *See also* Conn Smythe Trophy
Soviet Union (USSR) (national team), 49-52, 53, 60, 61, 63, 67-68.
    See also Russia
St. Michael's College School, 44, 45
St. Pats (Toronto), 28
Stanley, Allan, 42, 44, 47
Stanley, Isobel, 8
Stanley, Lord (Governor General) 7, 8, 9
Stanley Cup, 8, 9, 10, 11, 13, 14, 15, 16, 17, 19, 21, 22, 27, 28, 29, 31, 32, 33, 35, 36, 38, 41, 42, 43, 46, 47, 51, 54, 57, 59, 60, 61, 62, 63, 66, 68, 70, 71, 77
Starr Manufacturing Company, 6, 7
Stars (Montreal), 24
Stastny, Anton, 58
Stastny, Marian, 58
Stastny, Peter, 58
Summit Series 1972, 48-55
Sweden (national team), 23, 24, 61, 67, 73
Switzerland (national team), 23, 67

Tarasov, Anatoli, 50
Taylor, Fred "Cyclone,"13-16, 19
Team Canada, 49-52, 59, 61, 66-68, 73, 76-78
Thistles (Kenora), 14
Thistles (Rat Portage), 15
Tikkanen, Esa, 58, 62

Toronto Varsity Grads, 22, 23
Tretiak, Vladislav, 54, 55
Trudeau, Pierre Elliott, 49, 51

United States (national team), 23, 24, 63, 67, 73, 76-77, 78

Vachon, Rogie, 43
Vees (Penticton), 50
Vezina Trophy, 28, 43
Vezina, Georges "Chicoutimi Cuke," 28
Victoria Skating Rink (Montreal), 5, 7, 8, 9
Victorias (Winnipeg), 11

Wanderers (Montreal), 14, 15, 17, 19
Wickenheiser, Hayley, 71, 76
Wild (Minnesota), 69
Winged Wheelmen (Montreal), 8
Winter Olympic Games (1968), 45; (1980) 63, (1998) 71, 73, 78; (2002) 66, 73-78. See also Olympic Games
World Championship of Pee Wee Hockey (Quebec), 76
World Cup of Hockey, 60
World Hockey Association (WHA), 38, 51, 53, 58
World Ice Hockey Championships, 50, 53
World Junior Championship (1984), 65
Worsley, "Gump," 44

Yzerman, Steve, 66

Photo Credits